Theology
BETWEEN YESTERDAY
AND TOMORROW

Theology
BETWEEN YESTERDAY
AND TOMORROW

by (Joseph L.) Hromádka

Josef Lukl

Philadelphia

THE WESTMINSTER PRESS

Library of Congress Catalog Card Number: 57–9717

Preface

I wish to express my deep gratitude to the principal
and faculty of Knox College in Toronto for the honor
and privilege of delivering the Laidlaw Lectures of 1956.
The days I spent at Toronto were days of rich personal
experience. My lectures are nothing more than a con-
tribution to the present ecumenical and theological discussion. We have to think very hard and pray very ar-
dently in order to cope with the problems so terrifically
challenging our generation. It is my sincere desire to do
what is in my power to overcome all the prejudices and
barriers between Christians of the present generation
and to strengthen our fellowship of faith and hope.

> *Vexilla regis prodeunt,*
> *Fulget crucis mysterium,*
> *Quo carne carnis Conditor*
> *Suspensus est patibulo.*

J. L. HROMÁDKA

7

Contents

Foreword

These five lectures which were given by Dr. Joseph Hromádka, Dean of the Comenius Faculty of Theology, Prague, Czechoslovakia, constitute the Laidlaw Lectures at Knox College, Toronto, for 1956. Several reasons made it desirable that he should be invited to give them. First, as a distinguished churchman, theologian, and member of the Central Executive Committee of the World Council of Churches and a Vice-President of the World Presbyterian Alliance, as well as the head of one of the largest theological schools of Eastern Europe, he seemed to be in a position to give a unique and challenging, although not necessarily a popular, interpretation of theology in its relation to the ideological question. In addition, the various visiting delegations from the Protestant churches of Western Europe, Britain, the United States, and Canada, to the churches of Eastern Europe over the past few years suggested to us the desirability of re-establishing communications between these two sections of Christendom, despite the risk of misunderstanding.

Although the college and its faculty do not accept responsibility for the views that Dr. Hromádka expresses, and at certain points especially would disagree with him, we respect his sincerity and Christian devotion and desire to maintain that fellowship in Christ which with him as with the hundreds of thousands of other Christian people of Eastern Europe transcends such differences.

J. S. G.

Knox College
Toronto, Canada

1. Theology, Its Substance and Function

I. ETERNAL TRUTH IS CHANGELESS BUT NOT TIMELESS

We are standing amidst deep and unprecedented changes in the very structure of human society, both in national and international relations. In a later chapter we shall touch upon some of the aspects of the present era. However, right at the outset I wish to stress the point that our work in theology and the church has been shaken to its very foundation. We may shut our eyes and ears and ignore the critical situation in which we live. We may withdraw into the very sanctuary of our churches and lecture rooms, pretending that the turbulent upheavals and revolutionary changes of the present humanity do not affect in any way the substance and function of theological work. We may honestly think that the changeless realities on which our theology rests have nothing or very little to do with the problems, events, proceedings, and anxieties of the world. There is undoubtedly something permanent and unchangeable in the very objective of theological thought and in the message of the church. Over and over again a real theology goes back to some problems and issues that stay at the bottom of Christian thought and can never disappear beyond the horizon of theology no matter what takes place in the world or to what predicaments, transformations, and sufferings the church may be subjected.

And yet, it would be a fateful illusion to establish a barrier between theology and the world and to presume that a real theologian can possibly protect himself from the noise, tensions, and peacelessness of the world.

Anticipating what I shall later deal with, I wish to stress the fact that theology is in its substance inseparable from the church, being an essential function of the church. The church, however, is in its substance closely associated with the world; it lives at a quite definite place and in a quite definite time of human history. I wish to repeat: the church is by its very nature related to the world and bears upon its shoulders all the misery and sorrow, all the perversion, and also the radiant hope and expectation, of the whole of humanity. And it is the direct link between theology and what is going on beyond the boundaries of the organized, empirical church. What I wish to underline is the actualness of our theological thought.

The truth on which any real theology rests and which it interprets has nothing to do with timeless metaphysical ideas or with an abstract ideology. The truth of Christian theology can be preserved and understood only in its very relation to the concrete moment and place of human life, both spiritual and physical. A real theology is a constant confrontation of the truth from above with what is going on in human life. The truth on which theology is based is changeless, and yet not timeless.

The truth with which we have to deal is beyond all human categories, ideas, concepts, moral norms, and experience. It cannot be dragged down to the level on which we live. And yet it continually attacks man in his intellectual, spiritual, moral, and physical relations and only in this very attack and challenging power can be known, understood, and interpreted.

What I wish to say, right at the outset of my analysis, is that a real theologian must stand right on the ground of real, actual human life, of history and its events, and respond to the truth which comes as an inescapable voice from above. When I speak of the ground of real life and history I have primarily in mind the ground of the church living in the fullness of human interrelations. It is easy to concentrate oneself on the abstract ideal of dogmatic system; and it is easy to lose oneself in the currents of human life. It is, however, difficult to know about the challenge of the eternal truth, to relate it to personal consciousness and life, and, vice versa, to relate obediently all human personal and collective relations to that challenging truth.

II. THEOLOGY AND EXACT RESEARCH

Let us in a very brief way consider various forms of theological work. On the Continent of Europe, theology developed gradually into a part or department of academic, scientific system. Beginning with the era of Enlightenment, theologians, primarily of Protestant churches, looked at the church, its history, doctrine, liturgy, and practical activity against the background of human affairs. Christian faith became just one of divers forms of general religious life and was analyzed more or less from the point of view of human history, individual and collective experience. The essential ambition of leading theological minds was, for many decades, to apply methods of exact research, of psychological, sociological, historical analysis and understanding to any tenet of Christian faith, to its origin, development, growth, or decay. All the events described in the books of the Old and New Testaments were studied in the frame of universal history or at least of the history of the nations, peoples, and states between Mesopotamia and Egypt (or of the Mediterranean area as far as the New Testament was concerned). Similarly, religious ideas, cults, institutions, and moral norms of the old Hebrews were scrutinized in their relation to mythology, cults, and religious institutions of the Babylonians, Assyrians, Egyptians, and other historically perceptible tribes and nations. The same methods were applied to research of the New Testament, to the origin of " Jesus' religion," of the early church, of Paul's interpretation of the gospel and his missionary achievements.

There were deep differences between various theological schools in their understanding of the history of Israel and of the history of the early church. Some of the Biblical scholars interpreted the religion of the Hebrews as a by-product of the old Oriental mythology and civilization. Some were, in this respect, more cautious and critical, trying to understand adequately the unique characteristics and message of Israel, on the one hand, and of the gospel and the apostolic church, on the other. Some started from the analysis of the mythological forms, ritual, moral standards, and political institutions of the Oriental or (in respect of the New Testament) the Hellenistic civilization in order to understand the original meaning and nature of the history of Israel or of the apostolic church. Others started from the analysis of the oldest elements of the Hebrew faith and worship in order to indicate the more or less qualitative differences between Israel and other religions (or, by analogy, from the gospel of Jesus and apostolic faith in order to demonstrate the uniqueness of " Christian faith "). However, all of them approached the religion of Israel, of the Jewish synagogue, of Jesus, and of the apostles as an essentially human affair, as a part and parcel of human history, disregarding any supranatural or metahistorical factor which might have intruded and formed human life, thought, and history. Or, at least, any such factor was pushed to the very margin of the analyzed realities so as not to be permitted to intervene in the natural historical process of individual religion or religious community.

We may be shocked by various products of the research I have just indicated. However, before we reject the results of this type of theology we have to give credit to the tremendous work and achievement of a long galaxy of theologians engaged in the nineteenth and twentieth centuries in this kind of theological study and method. Many of the representatives of this type of thought were critical and skeptical, but some of them were very devout Christians. All of them were, humanly speaking, guided by an honest effort to get to know the real events of the history of Israel and of the early church as adequately as possible and to eliminate anything that might have darkened or even falsified the picture of the original faith and spiritual life.

We must never forget that the documents of the early times of Israel and of the Christian church are fragmentary and in many ways transformed by the generations that lived between the original texts and our present texts of the Old and of the New Testaments. We are separated by many ages from the days of Abraham, Moses, and the prophets, as well as from the days of Jesus and the apostles. The documents must be studied against the background of the days when they came into being. We cannot possibly claim to have an adequate understanding of them by simply reading their words, sentences, and paragraphs. The desire to penetrate into their very meaning and original structure is legitimate from the human point of view and it is legitimate from the perspective of faith.

What is real? What is truth? On what do we base our security? These questions are simply inescapable. Any honest man has a desire to know what is real reality and real truth. We have to think hard, to study and search intensively, in order to get at relatively reliable knowledge of the ultimate basis on which we stand and work. Just as we study nature in all its realms and aspects, in the same way we have to study history and primarily history of the origin of our faith, worship, and message. We cannot prevent anybody from applying the strictest and the most exact methods of research upon any event or aspect of the early Israel and the early church. After all, we are in all our doing part and parcel of human society. We are being shaped and formed by the society in which we live. The church has been always a company of real men and women standing on the earth, breathing the air of the time, and yielding, avowedly or unavowedly, to the impact of the moral, religious, social, economic, political atmosphere surrounding them.

A fearless and careful student of the Biblical writings can see the evidence of what I say on many pages of the Bible. The history of the people of Israel and the apostolic church is a continuous struggle and wrestling with manifold pressures and influences of the contemporary society. What is more legitimate than to study what really was going on in the days of the patriarchs; of the journey from Egypt to the Land of Promise; in the days of prophets, of Jesus and apostles? We must not ignore any knowledge offered us by human research studying minutely, exactly, and, in a way, mercilessly the interrelations between Israel and other Oriental nations complementing the information of the Bible by all attainable knowledge from elsewhere. In this effort we have to proceed in a strict way without premature recourse to what the ancient people called *deus ex machina* (let us note that this *deus ex machina* has nothing to do with the God of the Biblical message, although many Christians have very often put both of them on the same plane).

The history of Protestant theology in the last half century is a fascinating effort to interpret the message of the Old and New Testaments against the background of the history of religion, cults, legal and moral institutions of the old Orient (as far as the Old Testament is concerned), and the history and philosophical and metaphysical atmosphere of the Eastern section of the Roman Empire (as far as the New Testament is concerned). Many efforts of interrelation, comparison, and confrontation have brought different ways of solution of the very complicated and subtle problem of to what extent the Bible is dependent on the surrounding non-Israelitic and non-Christian world. There are theologians and historians like F. Delitzsch, M. Norden, H. Gunkel who have interpreted the Old Testament in the light of the old Orient, emphasizing the dependence of Israel upon religious, mythological, and other elements of their neighbors. There are others, like J. Wellhausen, B. Duhm, V. Rad, W. Vischer, who have on the whole insisted upon the uniqueness and spiritual independence of Israel. In the same manner run the lines of the New Testament research. There are men like W. Bousset,

R. Bultmann, Heitmüller, and to a certain extent also A. Deissman and J. Weiss, who point to non-Israelitic and non-Christian motives within the New Testament and the early church. There are, however, theologians like A. Harnack, P. Wernle, M. Dibelius, O. Cullmann, and others who question any decisive dependence of the New Testament upon the "pagan" world and insist upon the organic connection of the New Testament and of the early church on the one hand, and of the people of Israel and the Old Testament on the other.

What I wish to say is this: the great achievements of this method have to be taken into consideration no matter whether their underlying theology is adequate or not. The only way to cope with them and to overcome their dangers is to take them seriously, to study them, and to point by more accurate research to their inadequacies, shortcomings, and misconceptions. This type of theological work is not identical with what I call theology in the strictest sense of the word. Yet, it could be a fatal blunder to ignore, out of fear of critical method or by narrow dogmatism, what has been achieved by scholarly research.

III. Theology and Philosophy of Religion

Another type of theology we have to consider for a while is an effort to translate Biblical conceptions of God, man, and world into human categories or to indicate that what we call God is a consummation of supreme human ideas of truth, goodness, and beauty. This type of theology is nothing new. It is rather a constant, continuous trend going through the history of theology almost from the very beginning of the Christian church.

This very fact is understandable. Members of the Christian church have been living always under a direct or indirect pressure of philosophical and metaphysical concepts, of the milieu in which they were living. The words " god," " man," " soul," " life," " death " have been used generally by men of any nation or religious group. Ancient Greek and Hellenistic philosophers developed integrated systems of metaphysics in which the idea of god was identified with the supreme category of being, eternity, and rational truth. The subtlety and consistency of this way of thinking deeply influenced Christian thought. Through various underground channels it penetrated into the very fabric of Christian theology and gradually, very often imperceptibly, transformed the message of the prophets and the apostles into a metaphysical or religio-philosophical system.

The God of Abraham, Isaac, and Jacob, the God, the Father of Jesus Christ, assumed, in theological and even dogmatic thinking, step by step, essential aspects of the highest ideas of Plato, Aristotle, Leibnitz, Kant, Hegel, and so on. The temptation of metaphysics and philosophy is all the more unavoidable as the human mind is by its very nature philosophical. Philosophy comes from within, and any outward philosophical influence responds in a way to what is at the bottom of human mind. Every man is philosopher. Each one of us is bound by his very nature to be philosopher. Nothing is more natural than an effort to interpret Biblical realities of God and his Word philosophically and to transform them in a system of metaphysics. If we are honest with ourselves, we discover a stable philosophical temptation in the sanctuary of *our own* theology and in the pulpit.

This unceasing situation possesses its merits. It prompts us to think clearly, accurately, and distinctly. It prevents us from merging into vague formulas, fog of sentiments, emotions, and fantasies. Just because Christian theologians have been from the very beginning under the pressure of philosophical systems they were capable of elaborating profound, intellectually sharp, and persuasive systems of doctrine. Christian theology stood out on account of its mental clarity and depth. However, any time a theologian has forgotten the tension between the message of the prophets and the apostles on the one hand and philosophical motifs on the other, he has been found to lose the ground under his own feet and to get lost in the bottomless pit of speculations, in the cosmic process without beginning and without end. The God of the Bible has become an idea of his mind, deep, lofty, fascinating, to be sure, but an idea without fire, life, and love. Theology is essentially different from philosophy, even philosophy of religion. Theology, no matter how greatly it might be indebted to philosophical systems, is by its very nature a kind of contradiction to what we call metaphysics. The history of theology is a history of purification from philosophical infiltrations. All great theologians — Origen, Athanasius, Augustine, Anselm of Canterbury, Thomas Aquinas, Luther, Calvin — have to be scrutinized from this point of view.

We have today a special understanding of men who prematurely have died in the agony of this terrific life-and-death struggle. (Let me mention just two names: Blaise Pascal and Sören Kierkegaard.) It is no exaggeration to speak of the life-and-death struggle. " The zeal of thine house hath eaten me up." (John 2: 17; Ps. 69: 9.) It is a terrific wrestling between the God of Israel and the

Father of Jesus Christ on the one hand, and the gods of the human mind on the other; of the inward tendencies of humanity to get hold of the ultimate truth and realities of the universe. We do not despise philosophy and metaphysics. On the contrary, we have a very high understanding of all the efforts of man to penetrate, by his own power, into the deepest depth of the human soul as well as to the last principles and history. How could we forbid anybody to use his intellectual and spiritual capacities to know and to understand the world in its essential being and to reach the boundaries, the ultimate limits of human spirit, reason, and life, and of the world in all its dimensions? However, the testimony of the prophets and the apostles points to the Lord of man, history, and the universe who cannot be reached by any human intellectual or spiritual effort, who is beyond everything we know, and who breaks through our ideas and ideals, rational concepts and metaphysical categories, and manifests his glory and grace on the ruins of humanly construed philosophical and metaphysical conceptions of God and his being — on the ruins of our human pride, selfishness, and ambitions.

We cannot help being philosophers. Each one of us, whether he knows it or not, whether he admits it or not, thinks philosophically because the nature and structure of his mind prompts him to act in this way. Each one of us is continually being shaped by the atmosphere of our civilization, which is to a great extent also a product of human philosophy. Yes, indeed, many of us understand great doctrines of the church, great dogmatic formulas and creeds, as expression of *human* thinking about God, his work, and his ultimate purpose. Even we, theologians, in our pretended orthodoxy are under captivity of philosophical thinking. To be a real theologian is beyond *human* capacity. Blaise Pascal and Sören Kierkegaard may be mentioned as examples of the unbearable tension between the philosophical and intellectual nature of man, on the one hand, and the ever-growing awareness, on the other hand, that to know the real God and to be a real theologian implies a total surrender of oneself to Him who comes from the other shore of human existence, breaking our ideas and concepts of him, destroying our gods and idols, and irresistibly claiming to be the Lord in truth, love, and righteousness.

IV. THEOLOGY AND REVELATION

One of the great functions of theology is to liberate the Christian mind and life from the shackles of concepts and categories that have penetrated into the very fabric of dogmatic systems, of our preaching and our way of life. We live very often much more by human inventions and discoveries of what we call " God " than by the Word of *the God* of whom the Biblical testimony gives account. Hence we can understand the controlling and purifying function of theology. This very mission, however, can be performed only under one presupposition: that a theologian knows about the God of whom he has to speak. *How can he know him?* He can know him only if he goes to where he reveals himself. Where and how does he reveal himself?

The church from the very beginning of its existence points to the books of the Old and New Testaments as the only reliable testimony of God's revelation. This is an axiomatic assertion which cannot be demonstrated in any psychological, historical, or rational way. Here we are confronted by a real *crux theologiae*. It is a crux of truth and yet beyond any rational demonstration. It is a crux of contingency which marks the way of theology from its beginning to its end. Many a theologian has stumbled at this crux and broken down. However, a theologian who has gone to listen to the prophetic and apostolic testimony and who has been over and over again overwhelmed by the Word spoken to him personally has realized he has no other choice: *to listen, to obey, and to surrender to this Word* or *to turn his back to the living voice and to run away.*

At the start of the theological road is an *event*, an event between heaven and earth, between God and man, an event of a call, a personal call: make a choice, make a decision, take with mortal seriousness what I, the Lord of life and death, say and what I demand from thee. To think theologically is a matter not only of intellect. It is a matter of the whole human existence. All is at stake. The road of theology is marked by real mortal decisions, by struggles, by agony and victory. Hence we may understand what we have pointed to, that the primary task and objective of theology is to make clear that a right speaking of God is possible under two conditions: (1) that we speak on the ground of what he himself has said and done; (2) that we speak of him in a total surrender of our thought and life to him.

In present-day theology we very often hear of the existential character of faith and theological thought. It is a correct emphasis, since actually every theological adherence is a matter not only of thinking, but of the whole of human life. Just as the Word of God is an event, so also theology is an *action* of thought, *action of decision*, extending hands, receiving gifts of grace, and marching to the point of final destination. The term "existential character of theology" may have a perilous meaning if we deny the objective reality of the Word of God and project it purely into an act of the so-called human existential decision. Nevertheless, the term is justified if we understand theological thought as personal decision and act.

V. THEOLOGY AND LIVING INTERPRETATION OF THE WORD OF GOD

We have spoken about the contingency of the Word of God as a basis on which any real theology has to stand and act. It is a provoking assertion when we look at it from a rational and philosophical point of view. And yet it is the hinge on which the whole structure of theology revolves. But how can we really know the living God who transcends our human rational, moral, emotional, and any other capacity? We know him only *indirectly* through his Word and we know his Word only *indirectly* through the written letter of the Biblical books. We are not certain about the exact wording of the original Word and of the original written testimony. How agonizing is our endeavor to reach, through the present written translation of the Bible, the traditional texts of the Old and New Testaments and from there the original written testimony of the Word, the living spoken Word itself! It is agonizing and yet grand and worthy of sacrificing anything to reach the place and the time where the Word was spoken not only to contemporary listeners but also to all succeeding generations, down to our own churches, sanctuaries, and theological colleges.

We have to apply every human scientific, historical,

literary, archaeological, linguistic method to get hold of what the original Word may have been, how it may have sounded, and what was its original meaning. We are, later on, going to speak about the way in which the church has understood and interpreted the Word of the prophets and apostles. Yet we have at this very moment to stress the tremendous and almost unbearable responsibility of theology to struggle for an adequate knowledge and understanding of the original, burning Word spoken to the prophets, and of the apostolic vision of the risen Lord in whom the Word of the Lord of glory descended into the lowest humility of the Son of Man in order to liberate man from guilt, sin, death, and evil. This responsibility is not of purely theoretical nature. It requires all human powers and strains all human capacities. The responsibility is not only for *knowledge* and *understanding,* but also for relevant, challenging *interpretation.* What matters is not only to know, but also, *and above all,* to interpret it in a clear, understandable way.

This function of theology requires a deep knowledge of real men as they live, struggle, labor, rejoice, lament, and hope in the ordinary human life; in their human weakness and strains, in their sorrow and joy, in their grief and happiness, in their work and agony of death; in their childhood, manhood, and old age, in their defeats and victories, in their misery of guilt and sin, and in their ever-new effort to rise and to believe. A relatively adequate interpretation cannot be put into action unless we know the way in which children, women, men of any walk of life think and speak, know their manner of expression and means of personal communication. Theology extends its hands from the old ages of divine revelation in the history of the people of Israel and the early church down to the man who lives and dies today. A real theologian has to confront his knowledge and understanding of the Word of God with the ways the church has understood it. And vice versa, he has to confront the church, its institutions, symbols, creeds, preaching, pastoral counseling with what the prophets and the apostles testified about the Word they had heard and seen. Theology is a function of the church. At this point, we truly agree with many contemporary theologians who have stressed the church character of theology. A particular progress has been made in many theological schools of the present-day Europe, in that theology has ceased to be a purely academic, intellectual matter and has found its way back to the church and churches and congregations.

Yet theology has to understand the majestic sovereignty of the Word spoken through the prophets and incarnate in Jesus Christ. The sovereignty of the living God transcends all the boundaries of empirical churches and even of the one holy church (*una sancta*). The Word of God has relevance for all realms of the world, of personal human life, and of human society in its cultural and material, social and political, national and international aspect.

Our responsibility is closely tied up with the responsibility of the church. The church knows or it should know that the whole world is under divine guidance and destiny, judgment and grace, under the Kingship of Jesus Christ. Its noble function is to tell the world simply, humbly, without any selfish claim about the Crucified and Risen in the midst of the world and to interpret *this reality* in an urgent, burning way.

2. *The Church of Christ,*
Its Message and Mission

I. FUNCTIONS OF THE CHURCH

The problem of the church has become, in recent decades, one of the most burning issues of theological and ecumenical discussions. At the moment the starting point of theology was identified with the event and the mystery of the Word of God, the problem of the church assumed a new meaning and character. First, the institutional nature of the church was put under the judgment and transforming power of the living God, who has spoken and through his Word is continually present in the midst of those who have been called upon and rallied to a fellowship of obedient and joyful listeners. Secondly, the real church was distinguished from a purely sociological grouping of religious people. This is a signal advance beyond the situation of the days either of church institutionalism and scholastic supranaturalism or of purely sociological understanding of what we call the Christian church.

Now I could discuss the substance of the church under several headings. We could analyze the church as the body of Christ (Bishop Anders Nygren did it excellently in his Laidlaw Lectures — " Christ and His Church "). What is the relation between Christ's incarnation and the church as his body? Why do we speak about the flesh of Christ (*sarx*) to interpret his condescension and real self-identification with sinful man; and why do we speak of the church as his body (*sōma*)? This very question involves the deepest fact of the divine self-disclosure and the most subtle problem of the interrelation between Christ and his church. Jesus Christ took upon himself all the burden of sin and corruption in order to liberate men, to sanctify them through the Holy Spirit, to make them one body, one spirit, one fellowship, and to use them in the continuous struggle for his Kingdom. Yes, indeed, the apostolic message speaks with one voice about the risen Lord and his church, which is different from any holy place and temple, and which is ever under the transforming and reforming power of the crucified, victoriously present, and coming Christ.

We could deal with the function of the church under three categories: message or witness (*kērygma*), the fellowship (*koinonia*), and loving service (*diakonia*). In present-day theological discussion we invariably come across these three functions of the church. The church is entirely different from an organized society of religious people who proclaim some kind of religious or moral ideas. It has to carry a quite definite *message* entrusted to it by its Lord. It is a messenger, a herald of its King, proclaiming his living Word of redeeming grace and the Word of commandment. It is not master of itself. It is rather a voice of its Master, responsible for transmitting this voice undiluted, unfalsified, and undefiled by what men may like and dislike. The church is a *fellowship,* a visible rally around the invisible and still the most real Lord. Its fellowship is a constant testimony to the divine revelation and presence. It is not enough just to proclaim the message. It is essential to demonstrate the divine intervention in human life and history by an inward communion of human beings transcending all differences of race, sex, nation, social or political stratification, or the differences of culture and human abilities. Where men are . gathered together in their human nakedness, helplessness, and corruption on the one hand, and the new dignity and freedom on the other, only there can we speak of the church in its real substance. And the church is an *army of servants* forgetting their own interests and giving themselves entirely to the assistance of other human beings. The church follows its Lord, walks in his footsteps, and identifies itself with man wherever he may be: in the empirical congregation, beyond sanctuary, or in the most hideous place of the world. A member of the church has no right to look upon sinners in human secular society as upon lost sheep with whom he has nothing in common. He has rather to serve, to love and to lose himself in self-dedication and self-consecration.

We could relate, in a more traditional way, the substance and the function of the church to the threefold office of Christ — to his prophetic, priestly, and Kingly functions. This perspective would help us to understand the mission of the church in a very useful way. It would adequately relate the *preaching of the Word* not only to the prophets of the Old Testament but also to the consummation of the prophecy in Jesus Christ; it would underline the fact that the Word to be preached in the church is the incarnate Word. Furthermore, it would underline the priestly function of the church in a correct way, not as an institution of the priestly ordinances of the Old Testament or as a copy of the liturgical and sacramental mysteries of the Catholic Church; it would rather indicate the right attitude of the church to the world in pointing to the cross of Jesus Christ. The church has to take upon itself the cross, forget about its rights and privileges, and lose itself in the company of sinners. The administration of *the sacraments* is a figure and symbol of this glorious mission. The *Kingly* office of the church involves a victorious and joyful proclamation of the Kingdom of Christ extending to all realms of human life, embracing the universe and history and advancing to the ultimate victory. In this respect the church may be described as the army of the crucified King with the emblem of the cross radiating the triumphant hope and joy. The order and discipline commonly associated with the Kingly function of the church is much more than a code of regulations and disciplinary prescriptions; it is rather an expression of a free and jubilant self-discipline of the *milites Christi* who march forward, look at the end of history as the final victory of Christ, and who see also in Baptism and the Holy Communion the marks not only of the Suffering Servant but also of the sovereign, risen Lord. At the end of this chapter we shall complement or supplement what we have just said.

II. The Church and Tradition

All these aspects of the church have to be taken into consideration and discussed in our congregations, denominations, and ecumenical gatherings. The depth and breadth of the living church of Christ is unfathomable. They reflect the depth and the breadth in Jesus Christ himself. The present situation of ecumenical discussions characterized by a close concentration upon Christology as a basis of ecclesiology (the doctrine of the church) is certainly encouraging. I strongly recommend to all students of theology and any church member a thorough study of the issues indicated in the preceding paragraphs. However, I wish to deal with some problems closely associated with what we have just said but more pertinent to the situation in which we live.

We have pointed to the fact that the substance of theology is essentially linked to the Word of the God of Israel and the Father of Jesus Christ as we know it from the written testimony of the Old and New Testaments (of the prophets and the apostles). Now, there arises a serious question: How can we possibly identify the Word of the living God with the *written,* visible, and empirically knowable letters of the Bible? This is one of the most urgent and painful problems of theology. It must not be dismissed either by schematic and dogmatic definitions or by a radical denial of any superhuman factor within the Biblical message. It has to be faced responsibly and courageously. We do not know the Word of God beyond the written Word of the Old and New Testaments. However, we know that the written word reflects all the limitations, frailties, and weaknesses of man, of humanity. The written word is human (*omooycioc hmin*), subjected to the laws and imperfections of empirical humanity. And yet, this very written word is the mediator, carrier of the superhuman, living Word which breaks through into our human existence and life unprepared, unexpected, beyond any law of cause and effect, contingent in the truest meaning of this word.

Here I wish to make two preliminary remarks. First, the books of the Bible are by their human nature a part and parcel of world literature. We have no right to prevent the historians of literature, of poetry, drama, novel, jurisprudence, morals, or religion from studying these books with their ramifications in the human creative

mind. They are *classics* in a way similar to the poetry of
Homer, to the dramas and tragedies of old Greece, to the
works of Plato and Aristotle, Vergil, and Cicero. Such
study is one of the ways in which the great spiritual tradition of Israel and of the gospel has infiltrated human
civilization and contributed to a higher standard of life
and thought. We should rejoice at any effort on the part
of secular writers, thinkers, and scholars to evaluate
Biblical writings from the perspective of human culture,
literature, civilization, and *Weltanschauung*. A theologian has to possess such a spirit of freedom and sovereignty of faith that he fearlessly follows any human endeavor to understand and to interpret the Biblical literature by scientific, secular methods and from the point of
view of a secular thinker. The ultimate truth to which we
have surrendered can be at times darkened and misunderstood, but it cannot be silenced.

Secondly, the Bible of the Old and New Testaments is
a part of the tradition that is an essential part of the
church. Every church, whether Catholic or Protestant,
lives by historical continuity, and this continuity is identical with what we call tradition. It would be an illusion to pretend that Protestant churches are churches
of the Word of God without any allegiance to human
tradition. Very often the differences between Protestant
churches are due not to a different interpretation of the
divine Word, but to the weight and pressure of historical
background, to the differences of mentality, customs,
morals, and development in the past. The substance of
a Protestant church does not exclude a positive understanding of tradition or of historical continuity. While
we reject the Catholic doctrine of the apostolic succession, we do not reject the succession of faith or a loyalty

to the heritage of our fathers. The church lives continually by the fullness of her victories, achievements, and the theological and devotional richness of the past. All of us are deeply indebted to the confessions of faith since the days of the Reformation. It is part of our theological mission to study with a profound understanding the dogmatic, liturgical, exegetical, and homiletical tradition of the church in general, and of our empirical churches in particular. And now, I wish to point to the fact that *the written text of the Bible is a part of the tradition of the church.* This aspect of the problem was not revised and discussed in the days of Reformation. Recall what I said in my first chapter: We do not know the Word of God directly. We know it through the mediation of the written text (not to mention the translations of the Bible). And the written text has undergone a long history of transcriptions, revisions, interpolations, interjections, conjectures. The study of the text of the Old and New Testaments is a fascinating study. It reveals a loyalty and deep respect of our Jewish and early Christian fathers for every word of the Biblical books; but it reveals also many human factors which had gradually collected, shaped, and preserved the text on which our knowledge and understanding of the Word of God rests.

Here again we are confronted, dialectically, with the Word of God, which transcends human boundaries and acts in a sovereign way in regard to temples, churches, cults, priests, prophets, and simple believers, and with the text of the Bible, which is part and parcel of human tradition within the church. Being overwhelmed by the divine power of the Word of God speaking through the Bible, we certainly trust the divine Providence protecting both the original text against irreparable distortion and the ultimate reliability of the written word. Nevertheless, we cannot help stressing the human character of the Biblical text, and seeing in it a part of Jewish and Christian ecclesiastical tradition.

III. The Word of God and the Bible

How have we come to the close association (if not identification) of the Word of the living God and the written testimony of the Old and the New Testaments? We may reply to this question in a simple way: without the fellowship of the church we would not have taken the Scripture as the testimony of the holy sovereignty of the Lord of Israel, of the presence of the crucified and risen Jesus Christ, of the wondrous power of the Holy Spirit, and of the ultimate victory of Jesus Christ at the end of history. No matter how earnestly the church subordinates itself to the authority of the Holy Scripture, we must never forget that it has been only through the mediation of the church and in its fellowship that we are confronted by the Scriptures as mediator, carrier of the Word of God. Only through the church the whole rich literature of the Old and New Testaments has been given into our hands as the message of the divine acts of creation, redemption, and sanctification. The congregations organized by the apostles received the books of the Old Testament from and through the synagogue of the Jewish community. They accepted them as a promise of what had to be done and fulfilled through Jesus of Nazareth.

The apostolic and the postapostolic church collected the texts of the Gospels, The Acts of the Apostles, apostolic letters, and The Revelation of John into one book (canon) as the authoritative testimony of the Word of God incarnate in Jesus of Nazareth, of the new covenant replacing the old one. The Scriptures have been passed on by one generation to the other until they reached our own generation. Each epoch of the church has been formed by the books of the Bible. Each generation has listened ever anew to the Word of God and interpreted it to men, women, and children of its time. One of the most urgent and difficult responsibilities of the church has always been to draw a clear, distinctive line between the voice of the living God and various human voices and claims which have penetrated into the very sanctuary of the church. I call attention again to what I said in my first chapter dealing with the mission of theology. The real battle and struggle for a legitimate understanding of the divine message as over against human philosophical and religious ideas has been fought within the boundaries of the church, its congregations and sanctuaries. Indeed, theology has always acted as a vanguard in this struggle. But it has always depended upon the fellowship of believers, upon the living church, that the Scriptures would be preserved and understood as the Word of God spoken by the prophets and incarnate in Jesus Christ, and that the Bible would prevail against any misrepresentation, misconception, against the most profound human ideas and ideals. Theology may help the church; but it is the church that is, through its empirical branches and congregations, the very agent in the struggle for the clarity and the sovereign claim of the divine message. It is the church that has — speaking from the perspective of human history — maintained the books of the Bible as the only mediator of the Word of God.

The living God has spoken to individual men (Abraham, Moses, Samuel, Isaiah, Jeremiah, disciples and apostles of Jesus) with a definite aim and end: to form *a convenant with his people.* The Bible of the Old and New Testaments is a book not of individual piety; *it is a book of the covenant.* God, the Lord of Israel and the Father of Jesus Christ, proclaimed his will, his promise, and his sovereign grace to live in communion with his people on this earth amidst human weakness and frustration, sin and corruption, grief and misery. The essential theme of the Old and New Testaments is the story of the Lord Almighty, the triune God, eternal, omnipotent, righteous in grace and gracious in righteousness, descending from the glory of heaven and following sinful men who have forsaken the paradise and are ever since walking, stumbling, erring in their path of disobedience, yes, of revolt against him. I know there is a danger that whenever we try to reduce the manifold richness of the Biblical testimony from the book of Genesis to the book of Revelation to one single theme, we must never overhear all the voices resounding in particular books and passages of the Scriptures. Any effort of simplification or reduction must be continually controlled and corrected. And yet, I believe, it is legitimate to try in all humility to discover the underlying theme of divine history (and the acts of the Lord of Israel and of Jesus Christ are *history,* not a system of ideas or dogmas) as it runs through all the books of the Scriptures. It is the history of the Lord of grace and righteousness struggling in indescribable compassion, here on the earth, against man, for his (man's own) freedom and salvation; struggling, not only in empirical churches but anywhere else, with the disobedience and revolt of man; extending his hands toward erring, stranded, frustrated, and ever-revolting human creatures; proclaiming his holy will and, simultaneously, doing everything himself for the return of his prodigal sons and daughters into their Father's home.

We cannot deal here with all the aspects of the divine drama on the earth between the Fall of man and the Second Coming (ultimate victory) of Jesus Christ. We wish to stress only the fact that the church is in its very substance the instrument of this very divine action. In Jesus Christ, in his death and grave, the Lord of heaven descended into the very bottom of human misery and helplessness. The message of the cross involves the message of resurrection: it means that the shackles of sin, death, evil, and curse have been broken. There is no place, no matter how awful, dark, sinister, and cursed, where the Lord of heaven would not be present. The story of the Bible is the story of deliverances, of freedom and joy.

The church has a particular vocation to proclaim this liberating story not only to its members but to the whole world. It is possible to understand this history in its most profound meaning only in *a fellowship of believers*. This must be a fellowship where one member tells the story to the other, where the other responds, and where all the members, in penitence and humility, in liberty and joy, forgive one another, break all the barriers established between themselves, and render service of sacrifice, of self-forgetting love to anyone whom they meet. *The proclamation of the gospel in the fellowship of love and service* — this is the mission (and even substance) of the church. The church is a fellowship of men who have been called out of the world by the sovereign Word of

God, who have been made sons and servants, servants and sons of the Lord, who together in prayer, singing, and listening to the Word of God, continually renew, in the presence of the Crucified and Risen, their pledges of obedience and loyalty. However, it is the fellowship that transcends itself, looks continually beyond the boundary of its organization, proclaims the gospel of the reconciliation, love, and righteousness to every man *in the world*. It is a fellowship continually on the move.

IV. THE CHURCH AND THE WORLD

In conjunction with our discussion of the substance and mission of the church, we cannot leave untouched one urgent problem common to all of us, whether we live in the East or in the West, within the orbit of so-called Christian civilization or of the unchristian world. *It is the problem of the church in its relation to the world.* A Catholic conception of the church sees, in a visible, almost material way, the dividing line between the church and the world. Liturgical, hierarchical, sacramental orders and institutions indicate a sharp distinction between the sacred and the profane space, between sacred and profane acts. The church is — from this point of view — securely protected from the profanity of the world with all its temptations and evil powers by visible, sacramental, ritual acts and hierarchical authority.

Protestant churches differ essentially from this conception. They do not rely on any ritual, sacramental, liturgical, or clerical protection. They rely only and exclusively on the Word of God and on the guidance of the Holy Spirit. The dividing line between the church and the world is invisible and imperceptible. However, notwithstanding that conception, even Protestant churches have very often developed into ecclesiastical institutions and created an atmosphere of false security, on the one hand, and of a self-righteous, moralistic, and judicial attitude to what exists beyond the boundary of the church, on the other hand. A dangerous self-delusion has been created, as though a correct functioning of the church was in itself a safe instrument of the divine will and purpose, and as though the belonging to a church guaranteed a Christian character of the members of the church. Hence the peril of self-righteous moralistic attitude to the world in all its realms — moral, social, political, and cultural.

The prophetic function of the church undoubtedly belongs to its very structure. The church is responsible to its Lord to proclaim clearly and fearlessly the will of the living God. Obedience to Jesus Christ, the walking in his steps, and the challenge to follow (*imitatio Christi*), to act in the spirit of love and righteousness, is unreservedly the mission of any church. If the church would not speak and proclaim, who would carry out this awful and yet glorious responsibility? The terrific catastrophe of our era has shaken also the false self-satisfaction and self-complacency of the church and reminded it of its failures, negligence, tardiness, and laziness. The church did not speak when it ought to have spoken, did not call to penitence either its own members or the men responsible for human affairs. The church had readjusted itself to its surrounding milieu, to its social, moral, and political temper, to such an extent that it did not feel the urgency to speak for national, social, racial, and international justice, for poor, oppressed, neglected, underprivileged, forsaken people, before it was too late. At this point we find ourselves — wherever we are — in the same boat. None of us has any right to judge or condemn other men.

This prophetic message has been replaced by an easy way of self-satisfied moralization. The prophetic function must never be separated from the priestly function, that is, priestly not in the sacramental and ritual meaning of the word, but rather in the original Biblical prophetic and apostolic way. Catholic priests govern, mediate between God and man, perform sacramental acts. A priest, in the perspective of the gospel of Jesus Christ, takes upon himself the burden, guilt, sin, and corruption of the whole world, just as Jesus Christ did. There is, I repeat, an invisible line between the people of God and the world. And surely it is invisible; it is not in the hands of man to draw it according to human likes or dislikes, caprice, wantonness, and prejudices. The church is, through its members, so closely associated with the life of the world that we never can indicate where the line runs. The world rests and acts in our hearts, in our minds, in our actions.

Very often our membership in the church and our confession of faith is just a cloak under which we hide ourselves, cover our radically secularized souls. The world infiltrates, over and over again, our sanctuaries and penetrates even to our pulpits. Our preaching may sound pious and Biblical; but more frequently we use Biblical, anointed, and sanctimonious phrases as a camouflage of our own ideas, interests, and intentions. There is no human way to fix a definite line between the church and the world. We have to take this fact into very careful consideration. If we are inclined to pass judgment upon the world, we must first pass judgment upon ourselves. The world is within us, inseparable from our life. For the real church of Jesus Christ, there is no other way to carry on a prophetic message except in the way of taking upon itself the sins, failures, and blunders of the world. Jesus Christ identifies himself with sinners, publicans, harlots, Samaritans, and pagans; and he manifested the gravity of sin, darkness, and corruption by taking all that on his own shoulders, by giving himself as the living sacrifice for every man, whether in the church or anywhere else. " And, behold, the veil of the temple was rent in twain from the top to the bottom; and the earth did quake, and the rocks rent." (Matt. 27: 51.) The apostolic church broke down the barriers between the temple and synagogue, on the one hand, and the pagan world, on the other. (Rom. 10: 12; I Cor. 9: 20 f.; Gal. 3: 28.) This very understanding of the meaning of the redemptive power of the cross should help us to understand in a correct and responsible way our attitude to what we call " the world." We have to kill the very seed of self-righteousness and moralistic self-complacency.

But let us look at the problem from the other end. When we ask, *Where is the limit of our service in love and compassion?* we are not in a position to establish any point or circle where our service can end. Indeed, we have to do good to those who are close to us, in our families and congregations. Love as the gospel understands it is never abstract, but ever concrete and real. It starts with our household, neighbors, and co-members in our churches. But it is beyond human limitation. Jesus Christ walked at the margin of human society, cured lepers and cripples, ministered to the destitute and wretched, and had compassion for those who were despised and very often cursed and driven out of human society. He did not ask about dogmatic correctness, about church membership, about social decency, about whether they were believers or unbelievers. He saw *the man,* His brother, the son and daughter of his Father. He did not establish any ecclesiastical, political, national, or other barriers between himself and man. He acted in perfect freedom. He broke all shackles on the hands and feet of his people. In his sovereign love and absolute obedience to his Father, he carried the burden of grief and sorrow, of misery and poverty, of wretchedness and corruption, of helplessness and death. He was perfectly free man while he was nailed to the cross and when he was dying in the agony of " *Eloi, Eloi, lama sabachthani.*"

This is the way in which we have to see the relation between the church and the world. Without a joyful, triumphant understanding of the gospel of the incarnation, cross, and resurrection (which is the gospel of Jesus Christ's self-identification with a corrupted, wretched, and sinful humanity), we cannot understand the substance of the church and its real mission. The church as the communion of pilgrims has to be always on the way, resisting any danger of petrifaction and institutionalism. It has to see its own situation every day anew. The same message of the prophets and the apostles has to be listened to every day, every hour, every minute with open heart and mind in obedience and humility, and has to be applied to the time and place where it finds itself, where we find ourselves.

Where do we find ourselves?

3. *The Meaning of the Present Era*

Each one of us has come to realize the unceasing, almost volcanic changes in the very structure of our national lives, as well as in international relations. Wherever you happen to be you cannot avoid many discussions about the meaning of our era. We theologians are deeply interested in these discussions. Our work is closely connected with what is going on in our midst both in our churches and nations. Hence we have many conferences of theologians, preachers, and missionaries dealing with the predicament of theological education in the time of tensions. Every tenet of our theology, every effort to interpret the Word of the Bible, has to be related to the situation in which we live. Let us recall what has been said in the preceding chapters: The church of Christ is on the road, on the move, and the scenery on its way forward is changing from day to day, from year to year. The *same* truth, the *same* message, the *same* eternal Lord speak directly, in an actual, concrete way to man as he lives and acts. If we deal with the meaning of the present epoch, we do it not from the point of view of a definite philosophy of history. We do not pretend to possess such a philosophy. The danger of introducing a particular understanding of history into the realm of theology (including Biblical theology) is, to be sure, always rampant. None of us is free from the danger, just as none of us claims to be immune against philosophical motives infiltrating into the sanctuaries of theological wisdom.

45

However, we wish to say that our forthcoming analysis of the present era is nothing more than an effort to indicate some main characteristics of our times in order to make our theology real and to free ourselves from abstract theological speculations and fruitless moralization.

You will understand that the perspective I speak from is my own personal theological experience. But I wish to transcend this purely local or regional point of view and combine it with the world-wide ecumenical concern. Ecumenical theology is a living encounter between the churches. Furthermore, it is a living confrontation of the church (*una sancta*) with the whole of humanity. We have been engaged in many controversies about the church and churches in their relations to the events of present history. The deep division between the orbit of the West and the East, between the so-called civilized and underprivileged nations, has created agonizing problems of war and peace, of peaceful coexistence and progress of different peoples. At times, we are almost sure of the possibility of avoiding a new world catastrophe. And yet, the biggest issues of our international and ecumenical coexistence are by no means solved and settled. In a way, we are still standing at the beginning of the biggest ecumenical controversy within the ecumenical fellowship. Let me briefly list some salient aspects of the present-day situation as we see it in Central Europe and as many Christians all over the world have come to understand it.

I. The World Has Become One

The world has become one to an extent that it has never been before. Try to compare the civilizations of the Roman Empire, the *corpus Christianum* — society in the Middle Ages — and *the Western modern democracy* with the world of today; and you will understand the uniqueness of the present situation of humanity. Technical achievements and inventions, the rapid tempo of communications between nations and continents, the world-wide catastrophe of the last war, social and national aspirations grasping the imagination of the most backward nations — all that has brought all continents together and made them more interdependent than they ever have been. However, it is exactly this very fact that has caused perilous tensions and imminent dangers of explosion and self-destruction to the world. As long as the continents with their specific and deeply different civilizations or ignorance and barbarism were living side by side, separately, without common ground, the peril of the self-destruction of mankind did not exist. Since the end of the fifteenth century, the Western Christian nations step by step have been discovering new continents, exploring the hitherto unknown nations and tribes, and succeeding in establishing an international order which, however, did not penetrate below the surface of purely economic, colonial power strategy. And yet, an order came into existence. Western nations were so powerful that they became arbiters in the decisive moments of modern history. World War I was a contest of the Western powers for the leading authority, for equal participation in the international order. World War II was a continuation of the first one.

II. The World Has No One Arbiter

The second of the present concerns is the fact that the world in which we live today no longer has one single arbiter in international affairs. During the last centuries which preceded World War II, the international situation was given stability by the naval and political authority, wisdom and experience of the British Empire, plus American economic power, plus French military power. The Soviet Union during that period was at the margin of this international order; it was struggling for its own existence and survival; it was not an arbiter of the international ethos and order. Since World War II, there have been two competing centers of international order, Washington and Moscow.

We realize the dangers of this situation. It creates insecurity, uncertainty, and fears. The Asian powers, India, China, Indonesia, and other nations, have not as yet become new pillars of international order, but are gradually growing to maturity and coming of age. Western nations have lost their mastery of the world, and are since 1945 fighting a *battle of retreat*. The world order of the old type has disintegrated. The British Navy, the French Navy, the American economic wealth and ingenuity have ceased to be guarantors of the world order and peace, arbiters of what is just and unjust, what is for peace or war, what is equitable or fair, and what is wrong and fiendish. To assume that the present state of world affairs is due to some devilish intrigues, to the passion of some movements for evil, destruction, and violence, amounts to a self-deception. The history of mankind is, undoubtedly, a result of many mistakes, blunders, violent cruelties, and deceits. But one has, or we have — at the decisive moments of humanity — to examine ourselves and to ask what has caused our present predicament, why we are retreating from the leadership, and what one has (or what we have) to do in order to restore *our moral and political prestige,* our fair participation in world affairs. Small, partial victories may be won, the other side may for a moment give in — but the general situation of international life, and the distribution of power and prestige, is, at present, quite different than it was seventeen or twenty years ago. The Western world acted in a sinister weakness when it should have vigorously resisted the microbes of evil on the one hand, and of inertia and selfish calculation on the other. (Recall the attack of Italy against Ethiopia, the fall of the democratic Spain, the rearmament and aggressive interventions of the Hitler-Germany, without any serious effort on the part of the West to halt all these historically and morally disastrous events.) Furthermore, the orbit of Western democracy and civilization has not adequately and wisely assessed what has been going on in the other orbit — within the area of the socialistic revolution as well as in the old colonial and semicolonial countries.

The *retreating* character of the battle of Western civilization can be demonstrated on the occasion of almost any great decisive event in the international arena. May I refer, only on the margin of my talk, to what has been going on during the Suez Canal crisis? One of the leading English conservative weeklies stated that the Western public (statesmen included) were taken by surprise because they had not realized the profound political and moral change of the international scene. " Various forms of bluff, force, withdrawal of pilots, boycott, and sanctions have proved to be hollow. The only strong card in our hands is that Egypt needs huge sums of capital in the next ten years." Old-fashioned, Victorian methods do not work any more — " We should think boldly of different ways of reaching our objectives." (*The Ob-*

server, September 23, 1956.)

This does not mean the end of Western civilization, its debacle of defeat; this is just an evidence of the fact that Western nations do not any more command the leadership within international politics, that they do not shape and direct international morals and ethos. They are confronted by an essentially new situation which requires rethinking of many of their notions, principles, and methods.

III. The Insecurity of Christian Society

The world catastrophe beginning in 1914 and culminating in 1939–1945 was produced by ourselves, the so-called Christian nations. Forget for a moment that I come from a country behind the Iron Curtain. I speak with a feeling of Christian solidarity. We, Christian nations, have no right to blame anyone but ourselves for the last world wars. This is a historical fact. We may try to excuse ourselves, but we cannot escape our own responsibility for what has taken place since 1914. Is there, then, a certainty that, provided Christian society should prevail over against communism, this Christian society would be free of contradictions within itself? Would it be safeguard for the peaceful development of mankind? Are the Christian nations really secure against a new internal crisis which might plunge the world into a new catastrophe? European " Christian civilization " does not exist any more; the Constantinian or the Augustinian era is at an end. Theological students cannot close their eyes to this great new fact. " For I the Lord thy God am a jealous God, visiting the iniquity of the fathers upon the children unto the third and fourth generation of them that hate me; and showing mercy unto thousands of them that love me, and keep my commandments." (Ex. 20: 5-6.)

We, Christian nations, are responsible for the death of ten millions of men in World War I and for the death of possibly forty millions of men, women, and children, for many millions of tortured and exterminated Jews, during World War II. How deep has the responsibility for the misery and predicament of the present era penetrated into our heart and conscience? This is the most crucial question and the mark of this very question hangs over our heads, hearts, and consciences. Before we engage in a condemnation of non-Christian and anti-Christian peoples for the confusion, restlessness, and misery of our times, we have to take into consideration the terrifying historical fact of our own responsibility and guilt. We cannot strongly enough underline moral and political, social and cultural failures of the nations of what we call Christian civilization. There is no way out of our crisis unless we penitently look straight into the mirror of our own history.

IV. The Impact of the Socialist Revolution in 1917

The communist revolution is a historical event that has deeply transformed the very structure of European society. The meaning of the 1917 revolution is very difficult to understand adequately. It has so many aspects that no matter how we try to interpret it, we have a feeling that we have not got to its inner meaning. Many people call it " The Victory of Socialism," or " The Origin of Totalitarianism," or " An Expression of Russian

Imperialism or Nationalism." None of these " isms " get to the heart of the situation. One has to go to the Soviet Union itself to realize how inadequate are these various efforts of abstract interpretation. We invent some sort of formula, are happy about it, and assume that we have disposed of the fact. The socialist revolution of 1917 must be interpreted not only in political or economic terms, but as a basic event of the history of humanity itself. And that goes far beyond all our abstract interpretations. Should we not take into our consideration the fact that, in a way, communism represents a Westernization of the East? One additional comment: For the nations of Central Europe the days of Munich (September, 1938) were a turning point of history; I repeat: of history. The nations of Central Europe who were for centuries connected with the West have, after 1945, become part and parcel of the East of Europe. We do not overlook the tremendous significance of the fact that Great Britain did not go under in 1940–1941. We do, even at the present moment, feel deep gratitude that it did survive. But our people, after 1938, know that they cannot rely on Western nations, that they have to rely more than ever on the East.

What we very often forget to take into our consideration is the well-conceived plan on the part of European statesmen and some influential political groups, in the years of 1918–1938, not only to isolate the Soviet Union, but also to undermine and eventually to liquidate it. The Soviet state was from the very outset conceived as a thorn in the flesh of the civilized democratic society. Even in the days when it was tolerated and relatively recognized, the design of the world community without the communist society was never abandoned. The sinister years of nazism, of the Italo-Abyssinian war, of the tragedy of the Spanish democracy were marked by the intangible and imperceptible hopes on the part of non-Soviet Europe that the antidemocratic European states (also the states neighboring to the Soviet Union from the Baltic to the Mediterranean) might help to make the Soviet people impotent and an easy prey of future aggression. We may certainly mention many mistakes of the Soviet statesmen. But an anticommunist hysteria was one of the marks of the era between the wars and accelerated the tragedy of 1938–1945. That the Soviet Union found itself, at the end of World War II, in the heart of Europe, on the Elbe, was a result rather of the abortive anti-Soviet European policy than of Soviet imperialistic aggression. The victory of the Soviet Union and its ascendency to the world leadership took the democratic West by surprise and shocked the balance of its political thinking and action. The victory of the Chinese revolution 1948–1949 made the Soviet Union relatively invulnerable from the east and the south of Asia. The Korean War, 1950–1953, manifested the unlikelihood that the orbit of socialism could be undermined from the east. However, to do it from the European west — that possibility has not been given up. All the events at the boundary line between the East and the West of Europe can be adequately understood and assessed against the background of this situation. After one year of a relative relaxation of the world tension, we are facing another era of difficult and agonizing crises.

V. The Division of the World Into Two Orbits

We have been used to dividing the world into two distinct orbits, a totalitarian and an antitotalitarian democratic group of nations. In a way, it is understandable.

Ever since World War I, the political representatives, writers, and thinkers of the European and American democratic states were looking at their own states as a kind of pattern for other peoples and nations. We may recall the famous formula of Woodrow Wilson, " to make the world safe for democracy." From a political perspective, the Western institutions — political, juridical, cultural, educational — seemed to be a reliable safeguard of human dignity, freedom, and self-determination. Liberal democratic order based on public opinion, free press, free discussion, free criticism were considered the most adequate means and channels of human progress and development. After the catastrophe of World War II, the orbit of what we call liberal democracy has, all of a sudden, been challenged by an effort to organize vast spaces of the world on another basis, on a socialistic or communistic principle. We are going to deal with some of the main motives of communism in the following chapter. At this juncture I wish just to underline three facts of the recent and present history.

1. Let us remind ourselves of the crises of democracy in the years between the two wars when the democracy of Western Europe hesitated to make the indispensable decisions in order to demonstrate the vitality of its traditional system. This very fact cannot be forgotten. A searching question has disturbed our mind: Is the conventional democratic system capable of coping with the complex problems of the present age? The recent breakdown of the leadership of the democratic nations manifests inward weakness of the same system that a generation ago was called upon to organize the peaceful and progressive coexistence of nations and cultures.

2. A socialistic or communistic order of society was

not invented to impose upon men a new yoke of despotism and political tyranny. Whereas the fascistic movements in some European countries were designed to crush liberal democracy and to establish supremacy and dictatorship of the state, the socialistic efforts have been concentrated upon the consummation and more adequate safeguards of human freedom and dignity. Political institutions of democracy must be completed by economic and social liberation of men. The tragedy of the first decades of the socialistic reconstruction of Eastern Europe was a reflection of many aspects of the world after 1917: material exhaustion, civil war, foreign intervention, and a continuous threat on the part of the anti-Soviet Europe to isolate or to crush the Soviet people. The " cold war " has slowed down a normal organic and economically efficient progress of the socialistic countries and multiplied mistakes and political failures on the part of many socialistic leaders.

3. The appeal and attractiveness of socialism and communism for the old colonial peoples in Asia and Africa have been due to their design to help the human society *from the bottom,* through the economic and social liberation of the lowest and poorest strata of peasants and workers. What liberal democracy can achieve is limited, in those continents, to the higher, well-to-do, educated classes. For hundreds of millions of people, exactly that system which has been, in a derogatory way, classified as totalitarian tyranny, has been a step forward to liberty. We have to rethink all our schematic slogans and to give up the artificial division of the world. Especially we theologians must free ourselves from mechanically coined categories and schemes and look at the facts as they are.

VI. The Radical Secularization of Life

We are finding ourselves within a radical secularization of life. The advance of science, rational education, technical inventions, of film, television, radio, and air travel, of hygiene and medical care have deeply affected all humanity. The way of life and thought is undergoing profound changes. The secularization is extending to all, even the remotest corners of the earth, to all races and classes. The difference between the educated and uneducated sections of human society is in this respect waning. The human mind is rationally maturing and is more and more exposed to all the consequences of this progress. There is no way back. Nobody can stop the advance of science and of technical ingenuity, of education and culture. Have we realized what it all means for our material and moral life?

Secularization has brought many blessings in the realm we just pointed to. The epidemics are vanishing. Technical progress may provide more food and more comfort. However, we have a sinister feeling that our spiritual power is inadequate to cope with the results of scientific, technical and educational progress. There is a disproportion between our spiritual vigor and the energy of the present-day science. Tremendous efforts in almost all countries to raise knowledge and culture have, at least for some nations, achieved a very high level of material life. Yet we feel that the moral power and spiritual stamina of the churches are not strong enough. Some few years ago, Fulton J. Sheen pointed to this disturbing situation in his book on *Communism and the Conscience of the West,* saying that Western Christians have truth but no zeal, have the light but not heat, have the ideal but no passion. He also questioned the existence and the strength of love in the heart of modern educated, civilized Christians. I am not going to deal with this situation. I wish just to point to my own experience: the more we go to the East and meet men and women of the so-called Eastern countries, the more we are confronted with passionate convictions, warmth of heart, and joyful hope.

VII. Dangers in the Atomic Age

This is why we fear the dangers inherent in the atomic age. This is a result of divine providence and human ingenuity. Is humanity strong enough to check its inherent dangers?

The atomic age is, in a way, an almost automatic and irresistible consequence of breath-taking scientific research, technical inventions, and discoveries of human skill and ingenuity within the last two centuries, and primarily within the last fifty years. The two world wars accelerated the scientific and technical progress. The genius of destruction has always been stronger, more inventive and skillful, than the genius of the normal, quiet, constructive life. The atomic energy was first used for destruction and terror. But for this very reason we have to ponder the question whether the atomic age, in spite of its close connection with the preceding era, has not a qualitatively different meaning. For the first time in its history, *mankind has arrived at a possibility of suicide or self-destruction.* This is no exaggeration.

VIII. No Church Institution Is a Remedy for Secularism

No ecclesiastical institution, no organized church effort (whether the World Council of Churches or the International Missionary Council or other alliances) is a remedy against this new secularism. No artificially preserved religious institutions can possibly help. Some people in communist countries are happy about the " museum " or ghetto type of church, the church as a sort of " native reservation." But this is not a real church. The real, challenging question is: How can the church be a real transforming power, something much more than a beautiful decoration of life? What ought we, Christians, to do?

Let me close this section of my presentation by three remarks:

1. My own theology is strongly molded by what we call the eschatological motive of the Biblical message: The God of Israel and of Jesus Christ as the sovereign ruler of the universe and of human history has (not we), the reins of our life in his hands, in the hands of grace and judgment. He is in our midst, in the most corrupted, cursed, and depraved places, in all the remotest corners of our earthly life, yes, even in our graves. He is standing at the end of history, he, crucified, risen, and victorious, extending his hands to every man: the Lord of judgment in grace, the Lord of grace in judgment. No matter how deeply we may be interested in the affairs of this world, we nevertheless look beyond history and any human ideology. Our perspective is the perspective of faith, of the Biblical message, not a perspective of history.

2. Our analysis is just *a human attempt* with all its weaknesses and limitations; an analysis subject to discussion within a fellowship of the church.

3. No matter how limited our knowledge of human affairs and historical events may be, we have to take the

profound revolutionary changes of our times seriously. The history of the last forty to fifty years is a disastrous revolution on a world scale. Are we ready to learn its lesson? We are living in an era of severe divine judgment; but for that very reason, in an era of divine grace and promise.

4. Beyond Ideologies

I. THE CHALLENGE OF THE PRESENT MOMENT

The main intention of what I have had to say about
the meaning of the present era has been to indicate the
earnestness of the situation in which we live and do our
work. Just to avoid any misunderstanding, I wish, once
again, to stress the sovereign freedom of the church and
theology in regard to any historical event or any historical change. From what I said about the substance and
function of the church is evident my own attitude to
history. However, we have to take history seriously and
to understand the meaning of our own historical situation in order to get hold of it and to be free from the
shackles and fetters of history, in general, and of our own
time, in particular. Hence my strong emphasis upon what
has been going on in the recent past and in the present.
Have we not had the experience that a naïve or delib-
erate ignoring of what we call historical process makes
man slave of a historical situation, no matter whether
he knows about it or not? The message we have to carry
on goes beyond any historical or personal situation. The
church of Christ is a fellowship of pilgrims bound together by what is eternal and marching toward what is
beyond history. And yet, all believers, all the pilgrims in
any time, have been molded and shaped by external circumstances much more effectively than they have ever
realized.

Remember what I said in my analysis of interrelation

between the church and the world. The world in its historical moment has penetrated our minds, souls, beliefs, sanctuaries, altars, and pulpits much more effectively than we have been ready to admit. The world does not exist in an abstract way. It lives always in a quite definite historical shape. Understanding this historical shape is a precondition to understanding the world and men with their predicaments, frustrations, and hopes. And it is a precondition to understanding oneself in a more adequate way. The ultimate light we badly need for self-understanding is, to be sure, the light of the prophetic message and of the apostolic testimony. However, it is essential that we, guided by the supreme Light, try to observe with open eyes and minds the very events, the deepest changes, which have been going on in the recent past and in the present era. There is a real danger that we may halt on the surface of our social, public, or international life. There is a danger that we may not see the dimension of depth in the process of history and that we deceive ourselves, interpreting our present situation after the pattern of our traditional social and political concepts or institutions. For this very reason we are often unaware of the fact that our ideas, categories, and philosophies of life and history have become unsolid, sterile, uncreative, incapable of coping with the situation. What really matters is that we help one another, and see that no matter whether we live in the East or in the West we find ourselves under the challenge and pressure of the same historical situation, and that we have to know where we stand. Our present struggle and mission goes beyond any curtain, be it iron, bamboo, or golden, and beyond any secular or religious ideology.

To illustrate what I have in mind I may use my own

personal experience. As a young student of theology I lived still under the splendor and semifeudal glory of the old Austro-Hungarian Empire. I used to see the old Emperor Francis Joseph on various occasions, in all his monarchical majesty — on horseback, in funeral processions, in military parades, and on various other solemn occasions. His picture hung on the walls of our classrooms. Today my country, where I do my work, is under a communist president. What a great difference between these two historical situations, not quite a half century apart! The difference is not just political, external. It rather reflects the profound change, yes, even shift in the very structure of history. The events that have caused the almost abysmal transformation of our social structure, political institutions, mentality, and way of life have gone far beyond our normal political or other concepts. What is in the background of our present situation?

Here we have to probe deeply beneath the surface of our personal and public life and to ask what it all means for our decisions and actions. This question is very urgent exactly at the present moment when our churches and theology have been called upon to form a basis for mutual talks and discussion of the most essential problems of our life. We have certainly to create preconditions and prerequisites of a creative ecumenical *rapprochement*. I may be wrong but, nevertheless, I wish to express my misgiving about some aspects of our ecumenical contacts. Our brethren from Western churches and countries do not take seriously enough the new *historical* situation in the orbit between the Elbe and the Pacific Ocean. They are still under temptation to measure our social and political institutions after the pattern of

Western bourgeois democracy and interpret all the difficulties and predicaments of the so-called Eastern countries as a punishment for the new revolutionary efforts
of social and political reconstruction. They do not take
into consideration the fact that something historically
new has been started, and that the new efforts have to be
assessed from the perspective of global change, not only
from the perspective of Western society. Certainly we are
finding ourselves amidst a long process of profound social
and political transformation. Many aspects of our present life will be corrected. As long as there exists only a
minimum of international security and stability we are
bound to undergo many critical moments in our decisions. What is needed is to understand the new situation
in a constructive way and to struggle for the future without any thought of restoration.

There are many members of our Central European
churches who are confused, unable to penetrate into the
very meaning of the present moment; quite a number
of their ministers and theologians consider the present
social and political efforts as a temporary deviation from
the " normal " course of European history. They do not
evince any genuine desire to cope with the new problems
in a real theological way. They are waiting for a return
of the old days or for a more propitious opportunity for
the church, but in constant danger of being numbed by
looking back or by their hope to hibernate and to wait
for better weather. What aggravates their situation is the
fact that our Western brethren, visitors or observers at
a distance, look at them, very often if not invariably, as
true representatives of the church in its struggle for existence and freedom. They take it for granted that there
is no other way to bring the church to its real function

and mission except by opposition to what is going on in the area of the socialist countries. This is one of the most distressing aspects of the present ecumenical situation, more perilous than many a leader of the ecumenical movement realizes. Inevitable results of this state of affairs are both a growing confusion in the minds of those who wait, and a kind of complacency and self-satisfaction on the part of those who consider the situation of the old " Christian " nations as normal. Indeed, all of us have to be on the alert and constantly to revise our own decisions and concepts. What is needed, however, is a sincere and careful realization that — humanly speaking — the future of the Christian church and theology depends on our courage to take the revolutionary changes in the east of Europe and in Asia as an opportunity to make a new beginning. Very much of the frustration and lack of freedom some members of our churches feel and deplore is *due* to their unwillingness to take the present moment both as divine judgment and as a time of grace. Nothing more harmful can be done to them than to assist them in their attitude of negation and to give them a wrong consolation and a false hope.

The church of Christ is on the march. It is nowhere at home. It depends on no historical institutions and on no political system of liberty. It knows about the sovereign freedom of its Lord, who continually creates new opportunities and situations, even on the ruins of what had been dear to our fathers and to ourselves. He liberates the souls, ears, and minds of his people and makes them at home wherever he is. He may prompt his believers to revolt against many institutions and systems, but he also may help his people to work joyfully under new circumstances which may be at first frightening, and yet full of promise for the future. This joyful understanding of new opportunities has nothing to do with uncritical naïveté. It is more critical but also more creative than the observers from outside may be ready to admit.

II. THERE IS NO WAY BACK

Let me now go back to where I started my analysis. Standing at the crossroads of history, we have to deal with events reaching far beyond any external political or social forms. We cannot go back. Revolutionary changes going on through vast areas of some one and a half billions of human beings cannot be understood just as a result of intrigue, cunning, shrewd propaganda, and the machination of a small clique of politicians or conspirators. The changes have been overdue. The orbit undergoing at present a radical transformation of external institutions and also of its moral and spiritual way of life is identical almost entirely, or to a large extent, with the area of previously poor, hungry, and underprivileged people held for centuries in poverty, misery, and ignorance. Nominally Christian nations, or at least the ruling classes of these nations, have been responsible for the agelong misery of those strata of human society and of those colored peoples who are rising up and claiming for themselves a place of human dignity and self-determination.

The tragedy (although a Christian should not speak of tragedy) of the present situation consists of the fact that there is a lack of real, not just sanctimonious, repentance on the part of Christian nations. By repentance I mean a free and courageous recognition of our own and our fathers' and our forefathers' responsibility for what is going on not only in our countries, but in other continents. We are all the time on the alert to defend our way of life, our comfort, our riches, our undoubtedly great achievements of political and economic civilization. We are shocked by the fact that the most vigorous and far-reaching changes have been going on under the leadership of communistic parties and under the banner of Marxistic thought. Instead of asking, in a self-searching way, exactly why it is that communism has grasped the imagination and the leadership of the underprivileged, poor, and miserable people, we are trying to unveil any possible or impossible motive of violence, destruction, evil, and hatred on the part of the communists in order to ease our own responsibility and conscience. And yet the first precondition of our spiritual victory is, in my judgment, to understand the failure of the nominally Christian, rich, and civilized nations to assume leadership in the most decisive moment of human history. Many of the recent changes have undoubtedly been accompanied by much hardship, suffering, and violence. But can we forget that all that has taken place during revolutionary uprisings was greatly outweighed by the wrongs, injustice, exploitation, pride, and arrogance on the part of Christian civilized ruling classes during the last two or three centuries? Is our faith in Jesus Christ, the man of misery and humiliation on the cross, strong enough to make us give up all our Christian self-conceit and feeling of superiority? In our fear and horror of what we call communism rests much of our resistance against a real self-knowledge and repentance.

We cannot really cope with the situation unless we recognize our own Christian misery and responsibility and realize our solidarity with the communists in view both of the general predicament of present man and of the terrific challenge of reconstruction and the restoration of human living together, on a level higher than the preceding one. Christian theologians and members of the church have to look beyond present political systems and ideologies and resist any temptation to identify themselves with any one of them. Theology goes in its depth and breadth beyond any philosophy of our times, beyond " Christian " idealism or dialectical materialism, beyond Western existentialism or " Eastern " Marxism. Theology is, I wish to repeat it over and over again, no ideology. It is an effort to interpret, in an adequate and actual way, the Word of the living God and to understand the past, the present, and the future men and history in the light of the divine Word and the divine events. From the perspective of theology as we understand it, all human divisions, systems, social and political institutions, all philosophical thoughts, find themselves on the same level, on the side of the created world in its corruption and promise.

The dividing line runs not between communists and noncommunists. It runs between the Lord of glory and mercy, on the one hand, and human sinners (whether communists or noncommunists) on the other. Theologically, it is all wrong to see the main line of division between the Christian ideology and civilization, on the one hand, and the non-Christian *Weltanschauung* on the other. It is a real and urgent question whether any idealistic philosophy stands closer to the Christian faith and message than a materialistic method of thinking and analysis. The greatness of theology rests exactly in its humble and sovereign attitude to the present divisions between Christian and non-Christian civilizations, be-

tween Christian and non-Christian philosophies, between the Christian and non-Christian way of life. *Hic
Rhodus, hic salta!* What we need is a vigorous, courageous theology that goes in its depth and breadth to the
very root of our present situation and avoids any short
cut that promises to make the situation of the Christian
church easy and secure. What we need is a sharp intellectual insight into the very issues of the present era and of
the point where the church and its members have to wage
a real spiritual and moral battle for the cause of Christ.
Our spiritual and intellectual capacities are as a rule
not strong enough. And even those capacities we possess
are gradually withering away because of our unwillingness to see the real issues where they are and where they
can squarely be met. The older I am, the more grateful I
feel for the privilege of being a theologian and of struggling for a right, relevant, and adequate interpretation
of the Word of God and of the heritage of the preceding
generations.

We are standing within one of the greatest and most
responsible struggles with which the church and its theology have ever been confronted, intellectually, spiritu-
ally, and morally. The demands upon all of us are such
that we should forget all the fashionable divisions thrown
upon our heads by the political and public climate of our
countries and meet where the Lord of our life and history stands and opens our eyes to our mistakes, blunders,
prejudices, and to our great chance and promise. I hope
my brethren will not be provoked by my repeating what
I have already indicated: one of the greatest obstacles to
our mutual understanding and to our relevant message
to present humanity is an avowed or unavowed conviction on the part of many Western churchmen that

wherever a Christian church does its work adequately the orbit of the socialistic or communistic society will sooner or later be undermined and the nations living under communism will gradually return back to the field of " Western " society and its way of life. Any Christian opposition to " a communist regime " has been taken and respected as a real Christian witness much more seriously than any effort to understand the new situation after the communist revolution in a positive way, to give up any false hope of a reversal of history, and to ask what we can do in order to make the new society grow and to make a creative and real progress beyond the old social and economic order.

What I wish to make unmistakably clear is exactly this: the spiritual, intellectual, and moral tension under which we in our communist countries live, has in no way weakened our sincere conviction that our mission in view of our historical situation is positive, that the radical reconstruction of our countries is politically, economically, morally necessary, that we must not flirt with the splendor, riches, comfort, and freedom of bourgeois society, and that we have to realize deeply our solidarity with the peoples with whom we are, by the unforeseen course of history, closely connected. The future of the church depends — humanly speaking — on our positive understanding of our situation, not on any tacit intention to weaken the new social order. The prophetic mission of the church may be on many occasions a mission of protest and opposition. However, the prophetic function of the church must not be interpreted schematically only in this direction. On some occasions of human history the prophetic line may run in an opposite direction, especially when the majority of members of a church or the public opinion of the traditional Christian society live in an attitude of fear, resentment, and horror of what is going on in the orbit of social revolution. Especially today, in a time of danger, the churches are tempted to equate their liberties and institutions with the liberties and institutions of the so-called Christian democratic society. It may be our specific duty to warn against this misunderstanding and to underline another attitude to what is going on.

Speaking in this way, I try to do so as a member of the church universal, for the sake of all areas, not only for the sake of one (Eastern) section of the Christian community. We are responsible for one another. We must avoid any temptation to be partisans of one orbit of the present world. We have to listen to one another, to help one another. The responsibility of our Western Christian brethren to us who live on the other side of the various curtains is to understand our effort toward a constructive and positive understanding of the society in which we live. There is no danger on our side of losing a critical attitude to our social and economic order. There is no danger of losing sight of the dividing line between Christian faith and communist ideology. The real danger consists in a wrong, negative, sterile, and schematic view of the new society under construction.

III. CHRISTIANS CONFRONTED BY COMMUNISM

May I now outline in a brief way some few points of Marxistic thought that have proved to be helpful and fertile in our work and thought?

1. It has *related theory to practical life*. This is the real meaning of the dialectical method of Marxistic philoso-

phy. Any theory, any idea and philosophy, can be understood in its essence only if we understand the concrete situation in which it originated and if we relate it to our own concrete circumstances of life. We have very often forgotten the fact that any Word of the prophetic and apostolic message was an event in a quite definite time and space and that an abstract interpretation deprives the divine Word of its real meaning and relevance. We have also forgotten that the Word of God can only (intellectually) be known adequately, recognized, understood, and interpreted in its vital relation to our present human situation. We have been, by the tradition of the European philosophical thought, shaped and directed to an abstract theoretical understanding of the Biblical message and of the dogmatic tradition of the church. This same tendency has created an atmosphere of abstract moralism and judicialness. A Christian who takes his confession seriously tends to reduce the will of the living God to abstract moral norms and to lose sight of the situation in which a man lives and of what his real needs and conditions are. We have not yet overcome this tendency of abstract doctrinairism and cold moralism. Modern schools of theology have warned us against this danger, have underlined the vital dialectical nature of the Word of God. However, we have not avoided the temptation to convert the challenge of modern theology into some kind of new theological theories (the very term neo-orthodoxy indicates what we have just said). The different schools of Biblical theology have not had the magnificent effect of prompting us to relate the original Word of the prophets and the apostles to where we live and act. Even the famous " *hic et nunc* " (here and now) has become just an impressive theological *theory*. In the very substance of the theology of the Christian church rests the unity of theory and practice. There is no theology without an unceasing self-confrontation with what God said and did, with what the church has witnessed in its life and thought, with the needs, outcries, sufferings, and hopes of the present man. We have not time and space to deal with this problem at more length. Yet I wish to express at least in passing my judgment that the Marxistic emphasis upon the unity (not identity) of thought and life, of theory and practice, cannot be understood without the background of the Biblical tradition which has not died out in spite of all Christian intellectualism and dogmatism.

2. The same may be said of the *method of historical materialism*. This is, in a way, another aspect of what we have just indicated. Men and society find themselves in a dynamic process of history. Life is not static. Any institution, any aspiration, any achievement of humanity can be grasped only in its historical setting. Social, political, legal, cultural movements and institutions have always responded to quite definite historical needs, contradictions, conflicts, and aspirations. We have to go to the time and point of its origin in order to penetrate into the creative strength of any great political and social structure and to judge its real value. Many institutions and political forms of other systems of human society which have lost their function and vitality today or which have become obstacles in the advance of humanity may have had a tremendous meaning for human progress and welfare. It is our task, even today, to get to the real, burning heart of the old society, and in this way to liberate its original substance from petrified and ossified forms in which it has been decaying. And it is our

responsibility to look for new forms and institutions in order to preserve what was creative and powerful in the past.

Undoubtedly there is a danger of getting lost in historical process and of converting all moral norms into by-products of a historical situation. Furthermore, there is a danger of interpreting man and humanity as a moment of objective process of nature and history. Later on we shall deal with the problem. At this very point, however, I wish to underline the challenge of historical materialism, urgently important for our theological understanding of the basic issues not only of the history of the church, but also of the way in which the prophets and the apostles witnessed to the divine revelation. We have to relate the Word of God to a quite definite human and historical situation. When God speaks he breaks through human life. Something happens between heaven and earth. The message of the Old and New Testaments has to do with human history in spite of the fact that it transcends nature and history and that it cannot be interpreted exclusively in the perspective of history. Theologians and the empirical churches have always been tempted to reduce the Word of God, his redemptive deeds, to static formulas and to intellectual dogmatic definitions. Our exegesis of the Bible and our study of the life of the church have to take continually into consideration the actual situation under which the Word of God was spoken and dogmatic definitions, liturgical forms, and ecclesiastical institutions created.

3. Closely associated with what I have just said is the Marxistic emphasis upon the continuous danger of using high-sounding ideas and ideals as a façade and camouflage of human political, social, and personal privileges.

It has been a warning against self-conceit and the mystification of common men. Any movements of any institutions cannot possibly be understood, in their real substance, on the basis of the ideal proclamations and spiritual decorations or slogans under which they have been established and propagated. It is almost a rule that the most egoistic motives of various social strata, groups, and castes have been put into the most noble and idealistic wrappings. There is no social, economic, religious, philosophical, or cultural movement or institution free of a very cleverly hidden material interest. Marxistic philosophy claims to unveil the most reality and to free man from illusions or outright deceit. Marxistic leaders and thinkers maintain that Marx and Engels have introduced into modern thought and life an atmosphere of sincerity and openness. They have not pretended to be disinterested idealists. Their analysis of human history, of religion and morality, seems to be almost cynical; but they proclaim an intention to base all thoughts and action on what is true and real. We may have valid objections not only to the result of their analysis but also to the very method of their thought and action. And yet we cannot listen to them without admitting that our theology, empirical churches and their confessions, and even devotional life have never been free of material motives and self-interest.

4. We have been inclined to base human rights and liberties exclusively on *political* institutions and safeguards. We have introduced into state constitutions principles of human rights and interpreted what we call democracy in political categories. Marxistic philosophy of dialectical materialism has challenged modern liberal democracy on two grounds: (*a*) that it isolated an indi-

vidual man from society and distorted the organic community of men; and (b) that it made human freedom fiction because it concealed the fact that purely political freedoms may only deepen the inequality between wealthy and poor, satiated and hungry. Political freedoms without material safeguards and social equality are incapable of making men really free and providing for them all the prerequisites of human dignity. Hence the effort to transform the political democracy into a social democracy or, in other words, to establish a new, socialistic plane of human history. Here again we may point to some inherent difficulties of a planned socialistic way of life. But there is no doubt about the fact that the future of humanity cannot possibly be understood without profound social righteousness. The struggle of the truly underprivileged nations for a real democracy is unthinkable without a social transformation of their lives and without starting from the lowest strata of their societies. The present events in Asia and Africa demonstrate the tremendous appeal of socialism (if not communism) and the fact that a purely political democracy is incapable of solving the problems of these two continents.

5. Many objections have been raised against Marxism for having elevated the class war to the center of history and made it the underlying motive of social and political struggle. Without going into the details of the issue, we just point to the fact that the Marxists claim only to have discovered, but not to have invented, the reality of the class war. From the beginning of human history, there have existed class differences and the efforts of the ruling classes to govern the lower classes and to exploit them to their own advantage. The Marxists may have underesti-

mated other motives of the historical process: e.g., the motive of charity, the longing for righteousness, the message of the gospel. But the study of history, from its dawn down to the present time, unveils the dark reality of human exploitation and the privileges of wealthy classes which have been taken for granted without the remorse of conscience. It has been the intention on the part of the Marxists to eliminate the class war by abolishing class differences, by conquering misery, poverty, and hunger, and by constructing a classless society.

6. The very idea of classless society has been criticized by non-Marxists as either a revolutionary slogan purported to arouse revolutionary emotions and hopes or as a remnant of idealism which has illogically survived under the cover of historical materialism. It may be an idealistic element within the structure of Marxistic thought. In my judgment, it is a reflection of the Biblical prophetic and apostolic heritage, a kind of secularized eschatology. We may have many objections to the way in which Marxists try to materialize it. Moreover, we may point to a kind of idealistic illusion and self-deception on the part of the communists if they predict a social order capable of solving all, not only material, but also moral and spiritual problems. But the very idea of classless society does not contradict any basic motive of the Biblical message, just as the ideal of humanistic democracy may be regarded as a political, secularized expression of Biblical heritage. There is no question about the fact that the Christian hope, based on the gospel of Christ, finds itself on a higher level than any secular hope. A Christian believer has legitimate and unqualified objections to any effort to elevate secular hopes to the level of what we call eschatological expec-

tations of the new heaven and the new earth. But the very desire for a society without social classes, differences, and tensions is justifiable, indeed, higher than a purely political concept of free society.

What we have just outlined should help the reader to understand socialistic and communistic aspirations in a positive way. One of the American Roman Catholic theologians, Fulton J. Sheen, characterized communism as a passion for evil, destruction, and violence. There exists a tacit agreement on the part of many Protestant theologians, churchmen, and laymen that communism is the evil reality of the present era and that, however we may differ in our analysis or methods, we all have to concentrate our efforts to destroy it at its very roots. Let me repeat what I said earlier: any Christian theologian living in the orbit of communism and joyfully doing his work on the spot finds understanding and approval as long as his activity is regarded as an indirect but efficient way of undermining communistic society from within. But in the very moment that he accepts it as an imperfect but legitimate and morally justifiable way of human history, he is bound to meet not only disapproval but also a disturbed rejection.

One of our present difficulties rests in the fact that we have to deal very often with a dull repetition of some petrified proclamations and schematic definitions instead of a creative reinterpretation of the very substance of socialistic or communistic aspirations. Some people, even workers in industries and agriculture, feel tired of listening to many clichés repeated over and over again, without burning fire and inspiring force. Here I wish to call attention to our common weakness. Dead formulas and primitive simplifications with which we try to interpret ourselves and to understand the other side have made our discussions sterile and fruitless and weakened our own position of faith and action. Hence we have to re-think not only the big issues of our times but also the methods of mutual discussion and co-operation.

IV. CHRISTIANS CHALLENGE COMMUNISM

Let me now indicate the points at which we have to carry on our spiritual struggle with radical socialism and communism.

1. Speaking from a philosophical point of view, we may classify the theory of communism as a *radical historism*. It interprets man and society as a part of historical process. Everything is related to a historical development and conceived as by-product of the past and of the present objective situation. Dialectical materialism eliminates anything that could not be understood and perfectly explained on the basis of the continuous, unbreakable chain of the process of nature and primarily of history (the category of history is more important than the category of nature). Human reason, conscience, the very essence of man have no independent meaning. They do not transcend the boundary of historical process. They are part and parcel of the objective perceptible, describable, explainable historical nexus. It is here that our Biblical faith raises its objection and disagreement. Let me repeat that we cannot prevent anyone from a consistent scientific and historical analysis of any human fact, no matter whether we have to do with material or psychological and spiritual realities. However, what we call man, his personal identity and responsibility, resists any scientific, physiological, psychological, or sociological explanation.

Man is not only a part of nature and history, not only an object or a product of natural and historical process. He is an entity in himself, standing as a responsible, morally and intellectually active, creative being within the surrounding world forming his milieu, and directing the way of history. What we just say is not an expression of some kind of idealistic philosophy. It is rather a consequence of the intervention of the Word that comes from the Lord of nature and history. The challenge of the Word cuts across our human life, both spiritual and material. It is a reality inescapable, irresistible. It cannot be explained away. It has to be listened to, accepted, and obeyed. We have no scientific means to demonstrate the reality and validity of the divine call and of its irresistible challenge. But we know in the depth of our human existence that it is more real than anything demonstrable and explainable. This very call has shaped the history of man and thus, being beyond history, has been the most dynamic force of men and nations. It can be demonstrated only by personal witness and by fellowship with those who have heard and accepted this self-revelation of God through the burning fire of the Word.

Here we stand vis-à-vis a fact that is beyond any *Weltanschauung* (a system of ideological view of the universe and history), beyond any myth and mythological explanation of the world and life. To be sure, the witness of the Biblical figures (e.g., Moses, Samuel, Elijah, Isaiah, Jeremiah, etc.) was at the very outset associated with mythological and ideological elements. The history of the self-disclosure of the God of Israel and of Jesus Christ could not be isolated and freed from the time and place when and where it happened. As we have already indicated, the people of Israel and of the church of Christ have been, by the dynamics of their witness and by the unquestionable certitude of their faith, a creative force of history. The way in which the Biblical message has been carried on is not the way of discussion and intellectual demonstration. It is rather the way of witness and testimony. The struggle we are carrying on is not a struggle of ideologies. It is not our concern to establish and promote a Christian ideology against communist ideology. Our mission is a mission of faith and obedience to the living God. It is a mission that is equally positive and constructive in regard to the communist, and to any other human philosophical or political ideology.

2. We have to be clear on another point of our discussion which has produced much confusion and misunderstanding. It is the issue of communistic (or Marxistic) atheism. What is the real meaning of the atheistic aspect of the Marxistic philosophy and policy? Is it an organic and central element of Marxism and communism or is it just a marginal aspect of the Marxistic action? Many an outstanding theologian and churchman, even in the present day, assures us that the attitude of the church toward a communist society must be an unqualified " No " to it on account of the belligerent Marxistic negation of religion and the church. They take the atheistic, Marxistic propaganda as the essential meaning of communism and consider the communist society and ideology as an effort and perilous determination to exterminate religion and to construct human society on a fanatical godlessness. In this way communism seems to be the most sinister danger not only to the church but to the very dignity of man and the core of humanity.

We have to be realistic, open-minded and without any illusion as to the point we are just discussing. The situation of the church in any communist society is different

from that in a bourgeois or even feudal era. It has lost
its leading position, its moral and political authority. It
is no more confronted even with a climate of liberal
tolerance or indifference. Its very existence and message
cannot be taken for granted or — better to say — they are
no more organically part and parcel of the secular society. For many reasons the church cannot rely on any
official assistance and help. Its hierarchical or other traditional institutions have been closely associated with the
preceding structure of social and political life. In the
moment the church had been deprived of all old official
props, crutches, and scaffoldings, it naturally got uneasy
and tried to resist the new system and to look back nos-
talgically, to what had passed away. In many cases, representatives of the church became silent or outward sup-
porters of any effort to restore the old order. In this way,
the church and its antagonists have found themselves in
a vicious circle of hostility and misunderstanding, of misunderstanding and hostility. The church interpreted the
new society as an essential instrument of godlessness;
the new society felt confirmed in its conviction that the
church, by its very nature, is a force of reaction and vested
interests. In addition to that, an empirical expression of
the Biblical faith has been invariably connected with
old traditions, the mythical view of the world, and with
many superstitious elements. The communist ideology
and society claim to rest on a scientific rational knowledge, radically liquidating all the relics of the prescientific method of thinking, any myth and superstition, yes,
even any metaphysics that transcends exact knowledge of
nature and history.

Very often these claims of an exact method of thought
and research have been associated with vulgar, uncritical

simplifications of the results of scientific analysis. What was just a preliminary hypothesis has been elevated to an almost infallible dogma. Very much of the communist scientific interpretation of religion has been just an un-revised, uncritical perpetuation of the old "free thought" of the nineteenth century. Thinkers and scientists of the communist society have contributed a good deal to the progress of science and sociological and historical knowledge. However, on the point of religion, of the Biblical and Christian tradition, they have made little effort to go beyond what has been done by Feuerbach and the freethinkers of the nineteenth century. Hence the difficult situation as far as the discussion and mutual understanding between the Christian church and communistic society is concerned. Traditional churches have in many ways, by their actions and declarations, confirmed some of the Marxistic (and communistic) theories of religion and the church. And the communists, vice versa, have by their inadequate and very often shallow attitude to the essence of the prophetic message and the gospel proved to be mere antireligious propagandists without any deeper knowledge of the issue; they have not been able to win respect on account of their sterile and superannuated attitude to the spiritual depth of human life.

I am well aware of the difficulty of the situation and of the danger of being misunderstood or rejected by both the philosophers of communism and the theologians of the church. And yet, I dare to express my judgment that the meaning of Marxistic atheism is radical humanism. The center of gravity of it is not what we call negative godlessness, but an effort to free man and human society of anything that has crippled his understanding and his capacity to master the laws of nature, society, and history. Feuerbach and his most intelligent followers have seen in religion a *Selbstentfremdung* (self-alienation), self-delusion, and in many cases self-intoxication. All religious ideas, even the highest idea of God, are, in their judgment, man-made tools to escape the limitations, misery, and helplessness of human life by seeking refuge in the realm of an ideal but unreal world of enchanting illusions. They do not draw any line between religion and the prophetic message and the gospel of Christ. Christians have, by their practice and obscurantism, more than often, given evidence of what Marxistic philosophy of religion has maintained. And it is exactly here that we have to deepen our discussion and spiritual struggle with the communist conception of religion.

We have to understand that the atheism of *dialectical* materialism is a positive struggle for man, for his adequate self-understanding, for a better order of social and political life, for a construction of a society in which all class differences will gradually fade away. The dynamic force of this kind of atheism is not the negation of the gods, idols, pagan cults, and religious dreams rejected and condemned by the prophets and by Jesus Christ himself. We, Christians, are responsible for much misunderstanding. And we have to help the communists to understand their own antireligious critique more adequately, more constructively, and to free themselves from a purely negative, shallow, antireligious propaganda. If a Christian grasps the meaning of Marxistic humanism, and if a communist penetrates beyond all religious myths and superstitions to the depth of the prophetic struggle for the real God against gods and ideals, then both of them may establish a firm basis of a fertile, creative contro-

versy. We do not believe in any possibility of an ideological synthesis of communism and Christian faith. Such a
synthesis is impossible. They find themselves on a different level. However, a new atmosphere may be created,
an atmosphere of a right struggle for man, his dignity
and integrity.

3. In this way Christian theology and the church may
be effective in their struggle to safeguard man against the
tyranny of historical process and of any human social
and political order. The Marxists have the right to interpret man and his life as a by-product of nature and
history. We have to understand their emphasis as far as
it goes. We have to understand their goal to establish a
society of men liberated from the yoke of the laws of
nature and history. However, we must never forget that
the freedom and dignity of man are rooted in what is
beyond nature and history. Only as we penetrate to the
depth of this fact can we secure man against an outward
and a very subtle tyranny of the material world. No
idealistic philosophy, no pious phrases, sanctimonious
slogans, or anticommunistic crusade can be possibly effective and victorious in this struggle. The gospel of the
Old and New Testaments is not identical with idealism
or any sublime metaphysics. It is more *real,* more realistic
than any dialectical materialism. It reveals human nature in its glory and richness more radically and profoundly than a Marxistic conception of man. One of the
most outstanding Soviet writers, Maxim Gorky, once
said, " Man — it sounds proudly." At the bottom of all
the great communist writers and poets resounds an ad-
miration of man, a longing for his dignity, glory, and
freedom. But how can you secure all that if you make
man just a by-product of the process of nature and eco-

nomic development? On the other hand, the Biblical witness reveals more realistically than Marxism the sinister roots of human misery and corruption beyond the social and economic conditions of human life. It makes man in his deepest personal identity responsible for his failures, sins, and achievements without denying the urgency of the struggle for social, economic, and political prerequisites of righteousness, equality, and brotherhood.

4. Here we may touch upon the goal of the communist social, economic, and political planning: *a classless society*. In sober Marxistic thought it is nothing more than a new level of the social and political structure superseding the capitalist or bourgeois era of history. It is a program of social reconstruction and of political action, an effort to establish new institutions of state, jurisdiction, political representation, and civil rights on the basis of social (not only political) equality and of economic security. There exists no political freedom where man can be exploited and enslaved by other, financially and economically stronger, human beings. A Christian has no objection to this kind of social democracy. In many ways he agrees that a political democracy is not sufficient for securing human freedom and dignity. His criticism is directed against the idea that this society has a redeeming power capable of solving all human moral, economic, political, and international problems.

Yes, let us do our very best to construct all social and economic preconditions of a classless coexistence of men and nations. As long as there are deep differences between well-to-do and poor, satiated and hungry, noble and wretched, civilized and ignorant peoples, no real peace and mutual understanding between nations can exist. However, the roots of evil — moral corruption, greediness, hatred, egoism — go beyond social and economic conditions no matter how important these conditions may be. The reality of evil, of death, of grief and sorrow, of moral failures in individual life, in families, in the interrelation between man and wife cannot and will not be liquidated by the most perfect social and economic organization of human society. This statement has nothing to do with pessimism or with an indifference as to social and political aspirations of humanity. It is rather a sober realism urgently appealing to men to employ all the means of human spirit and body for the progress of society and to give up any illusions that might, one day, cause a tragic disappointment, cynicism, and frustration. An idea of a classless society capable of solving all the hitherto insoluble moral and human problems may be a dangerous myth, a by-product of an uncritical prescientific view of life and history. A Christian knows that even a classless society will be a society of sinners, of selfish, corruptible men, and that such a society will badly need the message of the divine grace, forgiveness, redemption, and self-denying love.

In closing, I wish to raise an earnest, mortally earnest question. Are we, Christians, ready to face the most difficult issues of our time? Once again: the dividing line runs not between communists and noncommunists. This line runs between the Lord of history, on the one hand, and human sinners (whether communists or noncommunists), on the other. We have to start a sincere and honest self-criticism. We have to look at the world of communism in the perspective of our faith in Jesus Christ, the Son of God and the Man of Sorrow, the Crucified and Victorious. And only then shall we understand our communist brethren in a Biblically adequate way. Have we an integrity of faith and a fire of love and self-dedication? What are we going to offer to the new society? This is the agonizing question of our time.

5. *Theology and Church*
Between Yesterday and Tomorrow

I. CHRISTOCENTRIC APPROACH

The reader may have realized that the main emphasis running through all the preceding pages has been the Christocentric view of the church and of human life. The perspective of Jesus Christ ever-living and ever-present not only gives us a right perspective from which to look at every event and at any problem of life but also makes us free, inwardly free, to cope with any situation without fear and without the burden of tradition or ecclesiastical and material interests. The Christian church is facing today a new situation. Let us realize what it means: that the leadership of the Christian nations is gone, that many Christian nations have become new mission fields, that the strategy of foreign missions has to be profoundly changed, that the classes hitherto identified with our traditional Christianity are gradually losing their weight and prevalence and that the working class, until recently pushed to the margin of human society and outside the influence of the church, is gradually taking over the responsibility for human affairs. Furthermore, let us once more see squarely the fact that the non-Christian religions are undergoing a time of renaissance and that the non-Christian nations may, before long (in the next generation), be not only constructive leaders or coleaders of the new international order but also

creative shapers of human civilization. This is no speculation. It is a dire reality. There is no use complaining,
recriminating, or whining. Still less are we permitted to
sit self-complacently in judgment over the godless world.
The time in which we live is a time of repentance and
witness. A time of repentance: to ask where we, Christians, have failed, what we have neglected, where we have
been disobedient to the heavenly vision (Acts 26: 19).

Let us forget about the divisions between the West
and the East, between the capitalistic and the socialistic
countries, between the churches this side or the other
side of the Iron Curtain. We all are finding ourselves in
the same boat sailing across a stormy ocean, often in fog,
under heavy clouds, without the sight of the polar star.
The members of our churches are confused, full of anxi-
ety, fear, and horror, under the burden of prejudices,
false propaganda, misunderstanding, ignorance of what
is really going on. The main question is: What *should*
we do, and what *can* we do, in order to make the situation better, to fulfill our duty, to implement our obligations? We are living in a time of witness: to go back to
the central theme and reality of the Biblical message, to
go there, where Jesus Christ himself stands, walks, and
acts. What have we that the world does not possess? It is
a challenging question with which our young people
are confronted. Our men and women are often dis-
tressed by the fact that our churches are soiled and pol-
luted by the same dirt and filth as any other worldly
institutions and citizens. All the more, they are perplexed
by so many instances of a real devotion, sincere conviction, and self-dedication to the service of men on the part
of secular men active in the political, social, and cultural
life. They cannot help asking whether there is anything

that makes a Christian or the church morally and humanly superior to the world. The burden of responsibility on the part of Christian nations for the calamity and suffering of present humanity weighs heavily exactly upon those of our young men and women who resist easy, sanctimonious slogans and look without self-deception into the face of reality.

Indeed, what is it that would justify our feeling of mission, that would make us certain that we can offer to the world what it does not possess, that without which it is deprived of an indispensable inward strength and perspective? Let us be true to ourselves. Let us give up any sentimental " Christian " pride and self-complacency. We are standing on the ruins of the old world and looking at a sinister picture of destruction and suffering. Our hands are empty, our hearts are shocked. Our souls are tired. Our prayers, sermons, and sacramental acts are accompanied by an imperceptible, and yet audible, sigh of tortured humanity, living continually under the horror of the last catastrophe without real peace of mind and body. We cannot claim that we represent a superior humanity and civilization. We may possess more earthly wealth. We may have a higher standard of living. We may be well fed, well clad, and perhaps well educated. The non-Christian peoples may be poor, hungry, living in huts, and clad with tatters. And yet, who knows whether exactly these hungry and poor people are not morally higher than we? Whether they do not represent a nobler humanity? This is the essential reality we have to face, and it is only against this background that we can possibly grasp the agonizing and provoking question: Have we anything that could justify our sense of mission and our urgent feeling of obligation and witness? It would be distressing if we understood this question in a purely rhetorical sense. It is rather a question of life and death. Without real and profound repentance, it is unintelligible and unanswerable. The answer is simple and yet terrible: We are not better, nobler, we are not more human, morally higher, more charitable, purer in heart, purer in spirit, meeker, more merciful, more hungering and thirsting for righteousness, more ardent peacemakers, and more suffering for righteousness' sake than millions and tens of millions of non-Christian men and women.

And yet, in repentance and longing for the integrity of faith, we may, I repeat, we may answer: What we have that the world does not possess is Jesus Christ. Have we him or, better to say, has he prevailed in his struggle for us? Have we opened the door and let him come in? At this very point we may once more understand the very meaning of the fact that wherever and whenever members of Christian denominations have come together in repentance and self-denial, they — after many discussions — have come to the conclusion that there is no other way to come together, to work together, and to offer a real service to the world (both Christian and non-Christian) apart from starting with the *reality* and the real *presence* of Jesus Christ according to the prophetic and apostolic message. We have to go *back* and, simultaneously, to look *forward*. We are indeed living in a time of great decision. If we do not give up all our futile and artificial divisions, if we do not gather as naked, miserable sinners around the crucified and risen Lord, then the day of tomorrow might be for the so-called Christian churches gloomy indeed. If we, in a self-complacent manner, look to the day of tomorrow, we may hear the outcry of the

prophet: " Woe to you who desire the day of the Lord!
Why would you have the day of the Lord? It is darkness,
and not light; as if a man fled from a lion, and a bear
met him; or went into the house and leaned with his
hand against the wall, and a serpent bit him. Is not the
day of the Lord darkness, and not light, and gloom with
no brightness in it? " (Amos 5: 18-20.)

It is only in Jesus Christ that we can see man in his
wretchedness and glory, in his corruption and dignity,
beyond all the divisions of race, education, social position, and political systems. Citizens of the so-called Christian nations and members of Christian churches have
failed to render a real service exactly in this respect. What
they have achieved under the guidance of the gospel they
have kept for themselves and used as a pretext for their
own pride, domination, and superiority. The time has
come for us to cease looking at man through our artificial
glasses and, in the presence of Jesus Christ, to see everything with liberated eyes in the light of him, the Son of
Man, who stands exactly where men stand, live, and die,
whether Christians or non-Christians, communists or noncommunists, white or colored, civilized or poor, hungry,
and ignorant.

II. SELF-CRITICISM OF THE CHURCH

Theology and the church as we understand them have
roots, bases, and ends beyond political institutions, social orders, and economic systems, but also beyond generally accepted moral principles and philosophical axi-
oms. And yet they act legitimately and effectively only if
they take the world in which they live *seriously,* if they
never forget that the *incarnation* of our Lord, his cross

and resurrection, are the points of intersection where the Lord of Glory broke (and continually breaks) through the horizontal line of human life — of the *real* human life. We do not know Jesus Christ unless we know him exactly at the point of intersection, at the bottom of the corrupted world.

Within the Christian church, there have lived and acted men and women with a singular charism of self-denial, of self-separation from the world, trusting only the coming Christ, the Holy Spirit, without any effort to influence and shape the world and society. Peace, non-resistance, penitence, sacrifice, quietness, the commandments of the Sermon on the Mount — these have been their guiding principles and obligations. Who could question the majesty of this charism? The charism of saintly self-denial and self-sacrificial love, of a total absence of any self-interest, of nonrecompense of evil for evil ("avenge not yourselves") is the glory of the church of Christ (Matt., chs. 5 to 7; Rom., ch. 12). I am happy to refer, at this stage, to the history of the Unity of Brethren (*Unitas Fratrum*) in Bohemia and Moravia, which was organized sixty years before the Reformation of Martin Luther, and the guiding message of which was an unreserved self-dedication to Jesus Christ, walking in his steps, rejecting any participation in worldly affairs, state, trade, business, court of justice, university, official church, earthly power, compulsion, vengeance, self-defense, and war. At the beginning of the Unitas Fratrum was Peter Chelčický (Khelchitski), at the end was John Amos Komenský (Comenius). They were different in their outlook and practical life, and yet both of them looked to the ultimate victory of Jesus Christ, distrusting the world, longing for the presence of Christ in human heart and life, proclaiming his commandment of compassion, forgiveness, and love as the only essential mark of discipleship and membership of the church of Christ. We can never close our ears to the challenge of what resounds in the gospel, in the early church, in various groups, religious orders, and sects of the Middle Ages; what is the underlying tone of all truly great saints, of the Reformation, of all the passionate protests against violence, compulsion, military service, armament, war. A Christian must never forget the invisible but real line between the church and the world.

And yet, the charism of self-separation *from* the world has been, at the highest level of the history of the church, very often supplemented by the charism of active responsibility *for* the world. The church of Christ is not identical with any company of idealists, perfectionists, noble moralists living in seclusion, dedicated only to otherworldly objectives. The church of Christ lives where Jesus Christ lives, in his humility and glory, glory and humility. He sits at the right hand of the God Almighty — and yet he is, through his Word and the Holy Spirit, in the deepest depth of human suffering, corruption, and sorrow. He is in the *midst* of human affairs. There is nothing in the world that could be unrelated to the real presence of Jesus Christ. The deeper and more vigorous the faith in Christ is, the deeper and more responsible becomes the attitude of a Christian and of the church to the profane world. We are not masters of ourselves, of our life and death. But for this very reason we are responsible, in the sight of the living Lord, for what is going on in the world, for continuous readjusting of our social, political, economic, and cultural life to what we ought *to be* and what we ought *to do,* individually and collectively, in the light of the prophetic and apostolic Word. There is no way of self-justification and of passing judgment upon other people. *We have to start from ourselves.* " O Israel, thou hast destroyed thyself; but in me is thine help." (Hos. 13: 9.) In a way, there is only one Person who is on the right side — the rest of humanity is on the wrong side.

What do we mean by these words?

Church history teaches us of a sinister temptation to identify the cause of God, of the Kingdom of Jesus Christ, with the empirical church, his truth with ecclesiastical doctrines and definitions, his will with traditional moral standards, his celestial power with clerical and ecclesiastical privileges and possessions, his ends with the victory of the visible church, his plans with earthly organizational projects, his authority with the canonical authority of the tribunal of a Christian high priest. There is going on a continuous relapse into the Judaistic form of religion: denouncing the enemies of an empirical church as enemies of God, proclaiming a crusade against them, dragging down the divine struggle against falsehood, evil, and godlessness to the plane of human ideological and ecclesiastical propaganda. This is an unceasing danger of many (if not of all) churches.

The Roman Church may be the most evident and visible example of the tendency I have in mind. The Roman Church is in a way a synthesis of some glorious elements of the old church, on the one hand, and of Judaistic, ritual, self-righteous security of Roman politics (hierarchical imperialism), on the other. Hence its crusades, inquisition, intolerance, and the ambition to be the only real church and the only legitimate representative of the commonwealth of Christ. However, we would be unfair to the Roman Church if we saw exclusively in it the incarnation of the sinister temptation of which we have spoken. A tendency to claim a monopoly in the representation of the cause of Christ rests in all churches. To divide men and peoples into two fronts: the one being on the side of God and defending his truth, the other one being against God, under his judgment, the incorporation of godlessness — this tendency runs through the ages, through all empirical churches. Especially in the days of great historical crises when much of our social, moral, political, and cultural heritage has been at stake, the churches and the so-called Christian nations have been tempted to interpret their own cause, the cause of their civilization, power, and way of life, with the cause of the church of Christ and with the cause of Jesus Christ himself.

It is here that we have to put our heads and hearts together and to purify ourselves of all self-complacency and moral self-righteousness and of avowed or unavowed earthly interests. To be sure, there exists another peril: to be artificially penitent in order to have an alibi, to preserve a weak tolerance without self-commitment, without martyrdom, without clarity, and without willingness to speak, to act, to fight. The church of Christ is a communion of *milites Christi,* who on their earthly pilgrimage testify to the truth and take upon themselves all the implications of their testimony and solidarity with men. Nobody can free us from the implications of real faith. What we call faith is much more than a pious state of mind, a religious mood and sentiment. Faith in Jesus Christ is a very serious self-commitment, a self-dedication to whatever the Lord demands from us. Our life, past, present, and in the future, is not in our hands. Our

earthly life — exactly in these turbulent years — rests not
in our personal decision. We cannot make any predic-
tion of what our present and future should be. " For none
of us liveth to himself, and no man dieth to himself. . . .
Whether we live therefore, or die, we are the Lord's."
(Rom. 14: 7-8.) This is what we have to keep in mind
and where we have to start from: *to look at Him,* at the
Lord of the cross and of the divine glory, and in his perspective to see ourselves and the world around us. The
faith in Christ is a combination of an unfathomable
depth and of a *free outlook of breadth.* The depth of
faith and breadth of love: the depth of love and breadth
of faith.

The Christocentric perspective, let us repeat, liberates
our souls, eyes, and ears from ourselves. The greatest
enemy of man is his own selfishness and self-concentration. A selfish man is slave of his own fears and anxieties.
He is unable to act freely because he thinks continually
of his own interests, possessions, money, prestige, comfort, glory, and material security. Salvation as the gospel
understands it is in the first place salvation of man from
himself. In the depth of human existence rests the root
of our sin. The very meaning of what we call sin is human self-assertion, revolt against any responsibility to
the Creator, Redeemer, and Sanctifier, against any obligation to men. At the bottom of *religion* is human selfishness. The most painful, difficult situations between
the God of Israel and his people come into existence in
the realm of religion, of false religion. " Ye shall be as
gods, knowing good and evil." Man wishes to be the
ultimate judge of what is right and wrong, good and
evil; he wishes to use religion and its cultic means to his
own advantage and goal. Religion as the expression of

human desires does not deny the existence of God; it
builds up temples, shrines, and sanctuaries; it invents
the most splendid forms and ways of worship. Alas, all
that for human ends! And such a religion gradually de-
teriorates into a most *absurd superstition* and obscurantism. It is revealing to what extent religion as a pious
self-assertion is closely connected with crass bigotry and
intellectual impotence. It is here that the most difficult
conflict between the God of the prophets and apostles,
on the one hand, and human gods and idols, on the other,
takes place. The main theme of the Bible, the theme of
the presence of the God of Glory in the midst of human
helplessness and depravity, is, simultaneously, the theme
of an uncompromising struggle of the Biblical faith
against human religion, superstition, and sanctimonious
bigotry. The revelation, the Word of God of which the
Bible speaks, is totally different from human religions,
cults, and myths. " Now therefore fear the Lord, and
serve him in sincerity and in truth; and put away the
gods which your fathers served on the other side of the
flood [river], and in Egypt; and serve ye the Lord."
(Josh. 24: 14.)

" *Eritis sicut Deus* " — and, inseparably connected with
it, the reply of Cain to the divine question about his
brother: " I know not: Am I my brother's keeper? " This
is our human situation. Self-assertion, self-concentration,
superstition and disregard for the neighbor — this is the
target of the divine attack and judgment. " Bring no
more vain oblations; incense is an abomination unto
me. . . . Your new moons and your appointed feasts my
soul hateth: they are a trouble unto me; I am weary to
bear them. And when ye spread forth your hands, I will
hide mine eyes from you; yea, when ye make many

prayers, I will not hear; your hands are full of blood."
(Isa. 1: 13-15.)

It is here that our great mission has to be carried on:
to confront the message of the prophets and the apostles
with our human religion and cult. We find ourselves in
the same situation as the people of Israel in the days of
the prophetic struggle, and as the early church in the days
of the apostles. Our churches and sanctuaries have been,
certainly in a noble way, corrupted by our pagan nature,
by our inborn religious instinct. The prophets warned
the leaders, priests, and princes against the holy places
of Gilgal, Bethel, Shechem, Shiloh, Beer-sheba — the
places clearly associated with some great names of the
past, but gradually transformed into places of superstition and official religion. The superstition and paganism
of our day is, needless to say, different from that of the
days of Israel and Judah; however, in its basic nature,
it is on the same plane. It is a great struggle, a peren-
nial conflict between genuine revelation of the real God,
on the one hand, and of the human religion, on the
other. The church and theology of our day have to understand the issue in its very depth and help believers
and unbelievers to face the challenge of the gospel, not
as an object of ideological debates, but as a life-and-
death struggle of divine truth at the bottom of our human existence.

III. Jesus Christ — the Hope of Tomorrow

Let us now once more summarize the main aspects of
the situation in which the church finds itself and in
which it has to carry on its mission. The turbulent process of postwar changes is in a way beyond our comprehen-

sion. Every year, every month, and every day confronts us with almost unbearable contradictions and tensions between nations, races, classes, power blocs, ideologies, and ways of life. Present-day humanity is longing and crying for peace, order, and mutual understanding. Wherever you happen to be, in every country, you hear voices of vast numbers of people, crying for a common basis of co-operation. And yet, there is no peace. After some few days of relaxation and hope, after a few moments when we can see the dawn on the horizon, there is a new storm, a new whirlwind, and new darkness. What to do in such a situation? We may be, and we are, in constant danger of cynicism or despair. We are in danger of rejecting or underestimating any human social, political, and international effort to overcome present dangers and to establish some kind of order, justice, and peaceful coexistence. There are millions of people who tend to withdraw from the complexity of human life, go after their own private affairs, and withdraw into their own heart and spiritual sanctuary. For several years we have been listening to a watchword: " Jesus Christ the Hope of the World." Is it a watchword of frustration? Is it a watchword of a pious soul disinterestedly looking at the world, condemning any human hope? There exists a tendency in present-day Christianity to understand the hope in Jesus Christ as a condemnation of human programs, projects, and plans. Let us not be deceived by pious radicalism; and let us look squarely both at the agonizing challenge of the human situation in which we live and, simultaneously, at our own failures and responsibilities.

We have dealt extensively with the present frustration of the world as a result of the past. Many words and passages of the prophets of Israel have become urgently vital for our churches, congregations, and individual church members. How deeply we today understand the Second Commandment! (Ex. 20: 5; Num. 14: 18; Deut. 5: 9.) How profoundly true are the words of Jer. 31: 29: " In those days they shall no longer say: ' The fathers have eaten sour grapes, and the children's teeth are set on edge.' "

It is one of those realities of human life and history that can be fully understood only in the light of the Word of God, and realized and accepted by faith. We are carrying on our shoulders the sour fruits of the trees planted by our fathers and grandfathers. This does not imply in any way a bitter condemnation of what our ancestors have done. We have no right to condemn. We have rather to understand what the solidarity between generations really means. It is a solidarity of sinners, a solidarity that in a way illustrates the message of what we call original (inherited) sin. Unless we see deeply enough the invisible channels of the failures and sins of our fathers, on the one hand, and of our predicament, on the other, we cannot possibly understand the big issues and problems of our times. All the divisions of humanity, all the manifestations of evil, injustices, and oppressions of our days are rooted in the past. They cannot be overcome as isolated facts and attributed to some single individuals or nations. Beneath the frustration of the present world linger sufferings, tears, sighs, and evil deeds of the past generations. We have to take this circumstance upon ourselves in humility and penitence. We have to listen to the divine judgments, which are severe and inescapable but also merciful and full of redeeming power.

What is, however, equally important is to realize our

present responsibility for our sons and grandsons, for the generations who will be heirs of our deeds, of our victories and failures. We are responsible for the future, for the day of tomorrow. This responsibility is no weak and fruitless speculation. It is, rather, a stark and terrific reality. Here we have to ask a question about the integrity and trustworthiness of our witness. Is it a witness of what the Lord of our life has entrusted unto us and of the real presence of Jesus Christ? Or is it a witness of our spiritual idols, human gods, of our own interests beautifully decorated by religious cults and pious words? Have we permitted the Holy Spirit to bring us to the living waters and to the burning fire of the divine revelation? To what end and goal do we cultivate our theological activity, organize our divine services, our liturgical forms and actions? Do we see the *man* to whom we have been sent as messengers of grace and judgment, of love and sacrifice? What effort have we made to find an adequate, intelligible, and urgent interpretation of the prophets and the apostles? Have we just engaged in a dull repetition of the old traditional vocabulary without being inwardly affected and burnt, cleansed and transformed? Have we gone through the fire of purification, of liberation from self-complacency and spiritual hypocrisy? There is no way of approaching the very heart of our generations unless we ourselves undergo a real suffering of repentance, of self-knowledge, and of a new beginning. Tremendous responsibility rests on our shoulders to get to know the Word of God in its burning substance, to understand present humanity, and to find a valid expression of what the Lord called us for.

We face a time when the *fullness* of the Old and the New Testaments is to be transmitted to our churches and individual members. Traditional forms of Protestant churches manifest, as a rule, a reduction of the Biblical message to some few doctrines. What in the old days was full of life and challenging power has become a collection of petrified formulas and moral admonitions. The testimony of the Bible is richer than what we call " the justification by faith only " or " *the soli Deo gloria.*" We have no intention to minimize these two great interpretations of the divine Word passed on since the days of Reformation from generation to generation. On the contrary, we wish to rediscover the original revolutionary depth of these two great definitions. And yet, we cannot help realizing that our theology and preaching, limited to the traditional doctrines of the Reformation, is inadequate. Millions of Christians in our countries have missed, in our denominations, the revolutionary dynamics of the old sects, Anabaptists and other movements, for whom the Kingdom and Kingship of Jesus Christ transcended the boundaries of organized church institutions, liturgical and sacramental forms. We have to rethink the ways in which Baptism and the Holy Communion have been celebrated. Very much of what was, in the old church, a burning expression of the present Lord, crucified and risen, and of the church as the living body of Jesus Christ, has been transformed into sterile customs and traditions without meaning and without a real function. The empirical churches have become a kind of museum and archaeological exhibit or, at the best, beautiful gardens with artificial paths and decorative flowers and trees. The churches have decayed and become part and parcel of our civilization. Instead of being a continuous, burning challenge, they have been transformed into religious clubs and " spiritual " appendixes to secular, social life. Hence we face the disturbing fact that millions of restless, hungry, and thirsty souls in the lower strata of our society look for help not to our organized, fashionable congregations but to small groups and sects where there is a profound expectation of new miracles performed by the Word of God. In these groups, there is a longing for the *fullness* of the Holy Spirit breaking through the traditional style of our church life, disrupting the boundaries of our conventional Christendom, and manifesting itself in what has been unexpected, provoking and offending the good taste of normal, decent Christians.

We have to remember what the Old and New Testaments heralded to the world: that the Kingdom of the Lord of Israel and of the Lord Jesus Christ extends beyond the limits of the organized churches, beyond the temples and sanctuaries, beyond the so-called Christian society, beyond our church alliances and ecumenical organizations. The Kingdom of Jesus Christ is deeper than the deepest depth of human soul, and is broader than all historical churches and sects together. The Kingdom of Christ embraces also those nations and countries where the name of Christ has not yet been heard, but where his sovereign grace may perform miracles hitherto unseen and unheard of. The Kingdom of Christ is the Kingdom of what is humanly impossible and inconceivable. Just as in the days of Jesus Christ, even today he may give a command: " Go out quickly to the streets and lanes of the city, and bring in the poor and maimed and blind and lame. . . . Go out to the highways and hedges, and compel people to come in " (Luke 14: 21-22). Let us take these words seriously and translate them into realities of the present day. Where are the poor, the maimed, the blind, the lame? Are they not the people who, from the Christian traditional point of view, are unworthy of a decent spiritual fellowship? Who are the lepers of our days? Where are, today, the men and women abhorred in the days of Christ, ejected out of human society, driven out into a cursed isolation? Let us not forget that the Lord may at any time make the new beginning (Isa. 65: 1: " I was ready to be sought by those who did not ask for me; I was ready to be found by those who did not seek me. I said, ' Here am I, here am I,' to a nation that did not call on my name ") .

Speaking about the day of tomorrow, we must certainly expect what we have not expected, hope to see what is unbelievable, and in repentance be prepared to see the divine miracles exactly where we today see only a desert, a bare land of unbelief and of atheism. The Lord who is present in the midst of our churches, finding only lukewarm hearts and fruitless religious habits and ritual performances, may turn his face from us to quite another direction than where we have hitherto been looking. It is really a terrifying time of judgment. But it is not too late. It is equally a time of promise. Are we ready to bow our heads before his seat of judgment? Are we ready to repent? Are we ready to expect new miracles at the most improbable places and under most incredible circumstances? Do we today take seriously the fashionable watchword " Jesus Christ the Hope of the World," or is it just a pious, sentimental slogan? Are we ready to receive him at any cost? No matter how humiliated we might be? Are we ready to pray in repentance and also in jubilant hope: " Amen. Come, Lord Jesus! " (Rev. 22: 20) ?

Let us repeat: the day of tomorrow is not in our hands;

the day of tomorrow is in His hands — in the hands of the Crucified and Risen. Only if we think of him, if we pray to him, if we put all our expectations upon him, if we forget our privileges, advantages, self-interests, all our human safeguards, only then we can creatively and hopefully work for the church of tomorrow.